A NATION WITHIN A NATION

*My deepest gratitude
to Raymundo DeAndrade for his guidance and wisdom;*

*to Chryse Gibson, Jean Lapointe, Victor DaRosa
and the staff of OXFAM-Canada
for influencing the direction of this book;*

*to the memory of François Moreau
who encouraged me to publish this book;*

*to Paul Mably, Nevin Orange, and Meredith Taylor
for their editing and comments;*

and last, but not least, to my family and friends.

A NATION WITHIN A NATION
Dependency and the Cree

Marie-Anik Gagné

Montréal/New York
London

Copyright © 1994 BLACK ROSE BOOKS LTD.

No part of this book may be reproduced or transmitted in any form, by any means — electronic or mechanical, including photocopying and recording, or by any information storage or retrieval system — without written permission from the publisher, or, in the case of photocopying or other reprographic copying, a license from the Canadian Reprography Collective, with the exception of brief passages quoted by a reviewer in a newspaper or magazine.

BLACK ROSE BOOKS No. X215
Hardcover ISBN 1-551640-13-9
Paperback ISBN 1-551640-12-0

Canadian Cataloguing in Publication Data

Gagné, Marie-Anik, 1967–
A nation within a nation: dependency and the Cree

Includes bibliographical references.
ISBN 1-551640-13-9 (bound)
ISBN 1-551640-12-0 (pbk.)

1. Native peoples—Canada—Government relations. 2. Native peoples—Canada—Land tenure. 3. Native peoples—Canada—Economic conditions. 4. Cree Indians—Government relations. 5. Cree Indians—Politics and government. 6. Indians of North America—James Bay Region (Ont. and Quebec)—Government relations. 7. Indians of North America—James Bay Hydroelectric Project. I. Title.

E78.C2G34   1994   323.1'197071   C94-900629-7

Cover Design: Rasa Pavilanis

Mailing Address

BLACK ROSE BOOKS	BLACK ROSE BOOKS
C.P. 1258	340 Nagel Drive
Succ. Place du Parc	Cheektowaga, New York
Montréal, Québec	14225 USA
H2W 2R3 Canada	

Printed in Canada
A publication of the Institute of Policy Alternatives of Montréal
(IPAM)

Contents

Introduction: French versus English Canada		1
1.	The Dependency Theory	5
2.	Becoming a Periphery: The James Bay Cree from 1600-1920	27
3.	Effects of Dependency: First Nations in Canada	53
4.	The Centre Exploiting the Hinterland: The James Bay Hydroelectric Project	109
Conclusion: Solutions		139
Map 1: The James Bay Project		150
Map 2: The Quebec-Labrador Peninsula		151
Bibliography		152
Index		159

Introduction

French versus English Canada

First Nations in Canada and around the world are often in conflict situations with their governments. When Europeans began to take over the newly "discovered" country centuries ago, something happened that they didn't expect: the First Nations Citizens didn't vanish. Instead, hostilities grew. Many people have difficulty understanding these disagreements, and the lack of information in daily news reports makes them unable to truly grasp the debates. This book provides a base that is required to understand the conflicts of First Nations across Canada, particularly those of the James Bay Cree.

I decided to narrow the subject to the First Nations residing within Québec's boundaries. I set this limit after reading Robin Philpot's book *Oka: dernier alibi du Canada anglais*, in which he asserts that the Oka crisis could not have happened in any other province. The crisis was directly related to the failure of the Meech Lake Accord and to the ongoing conflict between English and French Canada. A comparison of the English and French press coverage of the crisis highlights the differences of opinions: the English press generally criticised the Québec government, while the French press charged that the Mohawks were demanding too much. During the crisis, Québec was accused of violating human rights, by not letting food beyond the barricades and for beating the Mohawks. It is true that Québec experienced a tumultuous summer. Although conflicts involving First Nations have not been confined to this province, Québec's situation is unique in the country, since it is the only province fighting for independence and for recognition as a distinct society. Hence, Québec is the only province fighting against First Nations who are requesting the same recognition. This distinction led to a logical way to limit the subject, which otherwise would have been too broad, and from it the concept of a nation within a nation emerged.

The idea of a nation within a nation led me to investigate a link between Third World countries and First Nations and to make comparisons and interchange theories. I attempt to answer the following three questions: (1) Do First Nations Citizens in Québec share the same structures as developing nations? (2) Is there an underdeveloped nation within Québec's borders? (3) Can some theories that have traditionally been applied to the Third World be used in the analysis of the situation of the members of the First Nations in Québec?

This book was written in an attempt to try to find new solutions to old problems. If First Nations in Québec and Third World countries have enough in common, then theories relating to the Third World situation could be applied to Québec. Social, political, and economic programs could be exchanged between the two groups, and theories that have failed one would not be applied to the other. Most important, however, would be the possibility of broadening the base of support for First Nations in Canada, who are already reaching out to other First Nations south of the border, but who have not yet reached out to other southern populations. If First Nations in Québec are in fact Québec's Third World population, then links can be formed by creating a united front among those who suffer the most.

It's time to reach a solution regarding the domination of First Nations. It has become obvious that assimilation will not be part of the future. A grasp of the conflicts must be acquired before contemplating any solutions.

These conflicts are explained using the dependency theory. The "universality" of the dependency theory is the trait that distinguishes it from the other theories. It is universal because it examines the dependent relationship from all aspects of society. The interdependence of the political, economic, and social structures is analysed by looking at both the internal and external causes of dependency. It is important to note, however, that this book will examine only the external causes of dependency, because access to the internal causes is limited. In this paradigm, the centre is said to exploit the non-renewable resources of the peripheries, which are defined as having little control over their own destiny. The external historical processes that led the First Nations to become dependent on the centre are discussed. It is important to understand the emergence of the peripheral regions from a common history of imperialism and colonialism, but one should not assume that social evolutionism will someday eliminate all peripheral regions.

In addition, the effects of dependency on the economic and social development of a nation are examined through numerous data. Underdevelopment has affected income, housing conditions, levels of employment, violence, suicide rates, substance abuse, and health problems, and it has dominated the laws, politics, and educational systems of these dependent regions.

Finally, before looking at the possible solutions, the James Bay Project is discussed as a significant example of how a centre can dominate a periphery. In this case, the centre has dominated not only the environment but also the lives of the Cree. Many of the social problems outlined in the discussion of the effects of dependency can be directly linked to the James Bay Project.

I have divided this book into four chapters. The first describes the dependency theory in its several versions, including the interpretation I have chosen. In the second chapter, I describe how the Cree of the James Bay area have become dependent on the centre; that is, how they have become a hinterland. I discuss in the third chapter the effects of dependency on all First Nations of Canada, and the manner in which the political and socio-economic structures of First Nations across the country are harmed by this dependence. The final chapter describes, using the James Bay Project, how the centre can and does exploit the hinterland. In the conclusion, I discuss possible solutions to this problem.

In Boyce Richardson's book, *Strangers Devour the Land*, François Mianscum, a Mistassini hunter, was in court in 1974 before Justice Malouf. He was asked to put his hand on the Bible and swear to tell the truth, the whole truth, and nothing but the truth. The translator turned to the Judge and said: "He does not know whether he can tell the truth. He can tell only what he knows."[1] I would like to use these words, if I may, because this book is based on written materials only, most of which were written by "whites." This is my reason for stating only facts, and the reason why my suggestions for possible solutions have been directed toward the centre. I am hoping that by "telling you only what I know," you, the reader, will be able to deduce your own truth.

Note

1. Richardson, Boyce. *Strangers Devour the Land*. Douglas and McIntyre Ltd., Vancouver, 1991, p.46.

Chapter 1

The Dependency Theory

The "universality" of the dependency theory is the trait that distinguishes it from other theories. It is universal because it examines the dependent relationship from all aspects of society. The interdependence of the political, economic, and social structures are analysed, not only with respect to internal structures but also by determining the effects of external structures. Finally, the dependency theory is one of the only development theories which can be applied within countries, to different regions. It is a theory of development in the true sense of the word because it deals with the economic, political and social development of all countries and regions, and not only with the development of Third World countries.

In this book the dependency theory is employed to determine whether the Cree are an underdeveloped nation within a nation. This chapter is divided into three sections. The first discusses the emergence of the dependency theory, along with the definition of related terms. Other theories will also be examined within this first section. The second part of this chapter will determine the various economic, political, historical, and social forms of dependency. Other key elements needed for the dependency theory will also be brought to light. The final section discusses an application of the dependency theory to Canada.

The Emergence of the Dependency Theory

The Third World did not gain the attention of sociologists until after World War II. Before that time, most researchers believed that Third World countries would simply evolve as developed countries had, and that they were merely a bit behind. These scientists were social evolutionists, many of whom conceived of stages of development whereby one could look at a country's characteristics and determine exactly at which level of development they were. Spencer, Parsons, and Rostow were three of the most well-known social evolutionists. Rostow developed five stages of development that all societies had and would go through. Each of these stages had as a focal point capital accumulation and entrepreneurship.

Dependency theorists do not agree with social evolutionists, because they believe that there are internal and external factors that influence the development of countries. There are differences of opinion, however, among dependency theorists, some of whom believe that external factors are to blame, while others believe that internal structures are at fault for the state of underdevelopment. Allahar points out that dependency theorists who blame the internal structures consider development to be a phenomenon that occurs in the political and socio-economic structures of particular countries; hence, some countries move toward development while others move toward underdevelopment.

Although social evolutionists have been popular, there are also the dualists or diffusionist theorists. They believe that development and underdevelopment are completely separate issues, and they conclude that if regions are not developed it's because there are flaws in the internal structures of the periphery. Internal structures are the political, economic, social, and class systems of a periphery, and external structures are the international monetary systems and international political pressures. However, dependency theorists base their theory on the relationship that exists between the centre and the periphery. As Allahar states, "dependency thinkers reverse the dualist position to see the modern sectors as the main obstacles to development in the periphery."[1]

As one can see, there are several theories that were developed to analyse the state of underdeveloped countries. The dependency theory, however, is much more complex than the ones described above because of the extreme positions that are included within it. For example, there are Marxists who believe in economic dependence only; others believe that the only cause is found in the external structures; and still others believe the problem is an internal one.

Roxborough explains the complexity of the dependency theory by stating that it is a paradigm, not a single theory. Many criticise the dependency theory because it does not examine the development of Third World countries independently of the development of the North. Dependency theorists, however, see the world as a "single system."[2] They believe that one must look at how underdeveloped countries were "inserted" into the world system and research how their historical positions and development were different from that of the North. The dependency theory was in fact created in response to imperialistic theories. Roxborough explains it as follows:

> If an analysis of the relations between developed and underdeveloped societies that focused on the processes occurring in the developed half of the equation produced a theory of imperialism then if attention was systematically focused on the other half of the equation, the underdeveloped societies, a theory of dependency would be produced.[3]

Therefore, according to Roxborough, dependency theories try to explain the economic and social structures that are found in dependent or "imperialised" countries.

Definitions of the term dependency will enable the reader to gain a clearer sense of the variances found in this paradigm. Dos Santos defines dependency as follows:

> A situation in which a certain group of countries have their economies conditioned by the development and expansion of another economy, to which their own is subjected ... Dependency conditions a certain internal structure which redefines it as a function of the structural possibilities of the distinct national economies.[4]

Roxborough agrees with the definition put forward by Dos Santos, because it takes into consideration both the internal and the external factors of dependency.

Many criticise dependency theorists because they do not consider interdependent relationships. Dos Santos, however, does recognise the existence of interdependent relationships, but states that the relationship is dependent when "some countries (the dominant ones) can expand and can be self-sustaining, while other countries (the dependent ones) can do this only as a reflection of that expansion."[5]

Before venturing any further into the definitions of dependency and related terms, it is interesting to note the origin of this theory. Thomas Hall describes the emergence of the dependency theory as follows: "dependency theory was developed by scholars native to semi-peripheral areas. It did not become 'respectable' until it was 'denied' and taken to the core, where it was transformed into world-system theory and was reexported to the periphery."[6] Anton Allahar lists some of the first theorists who belonged to the "school of structural dependency theory": André Gunder Frank in the 1960s, Theotonio Dos Santos, Fernando Henrique Cardoso, Enzo Faletto, Celso Furtado, Ronald H. Chilcote, and Joel Edelstein.[7]

Dependency theorists use the terms "centre" and "periphery" to describe the developed and the underdeveloped or, to be more precise, the "controller" and the "dependent." Allahar quotes Chirot when describing the various terms employed to characterise the "centre" and the "periphery":

> The most developed countries belong to the "core" of the system, the "metropole" or the "centre." The least developed, on the other hand, are "satellites" that were forcibly brought into the "orbit" of world capitalism, and they belong to the "periphery" or the "hinterland" of that system. Finally, those countries occupying an intermediate position are variously called "semicore" or "semiperipheral."[8]

It is necessary to understand how underdevelopment is viewed by dependency theorists, since the causes of underdevelopment vary from theory to theory. It is also imperative to understand this term because, according to Rosemary and Ray Bromley, there is a direct relationship between the level of a country's "underdevelopment" and its dependency. The more a country relies on foreign investment, political decisions, resources, and technology, the fewer important changes a country can make without the approval of outsiders, and the more likely that the underdevelopment will increase. Rosemary and Ray Bromley conclude that because this direct relationship between underdevelopment and dependency exists, the level of development of a particular country lies in "the way which the country has been incorporated into the world economic and political system."[9] Before entering into a discussion of the implications of this statement, it is important to define development and underdevelopment. To begin, the emergence of the terms used to describe underdevelopment will be discussed. Following this is a statement from an expert from an underdeveloped country who expresses his preference of terms.

The terms "civilized" or "advanced" countries were exchanged for "developed" or "more developed" countries when colonized countries began to regain their freedom. Rosemary and Ray Bromley point out that the terms "primitive" and "backward" countries were replaced by "underdeveloped" and "less developed." However, many felt that these terms were still disrespectful, and hence the terms "newly-emerged countries," "developing countries," "Third World countries," and "the South" emerged.[10]

Francisco Sagasti, an expert from Peru featured in CIDA's series Path of Development, *Behind the Image*, identified many of these same names for underdeveloped countries. He elaborates by stating that the terms developing, primitive, and backward are offensive, because they suggest that these countries are following the same path of development as "developed" countries. Third World, the South, and underdeveloped are not offensive, because they suggest that these countries are labelled this way because there is a First World, a North, and developed countries. Therefore, the appropriate terms are the South, underdeveloped, and Third World.

Even though there are many trends found in the dependency paradigm, Allahar states that all theorists agree that underdevelopment "is not the original state or stage in which all countries once found themselves."[11] Dependency theorists believe that underdevelopment is a state that came after contact with imperialist nations.

Rosemary and Ray Bromley define development as "any process of gradual, long-term change in the conditions affecting human life."[12] Furthermore, they state that change is stopped because of the lack of resources, conflicting interests between the classes, and the history that lingers on to influence the present. The importance of a class and history analysis will be discussed later; however, the distinction between undeveloped and underdeveloped is explained by the Bromleys.

Rosemary and Ray Bromley make a clear distinction between the terms "underdeveloped" and "undeveloped." Development in undeveloped countries occurs while maintaining self-reliance. Undeveloped countries have easier access to development because they have self-reliance; they are not controlled by outside economic and political powers. These countries have not been colonized. Underdeveloped countries, on the other hand, are dependent. They have no self-reliance and need foreign investment and technology. Therefore, according to Rosemary and Ray Bromley, countries that are undeveloped can have access to development and have fewer problems with social and economic inequalities, creating a stronger balance.

For the Bromleys, self-reliance is the key indicator that determines whether a country or region is underdeveloped or undeveloped. This point will be of some consequence when discussing the Cree's self-reliance. These key indicators determine the degree of underdevelopment in a particular country.

The Bromleys state that the simplest way to determine if a region is underdeveloped is to examine its gross national product. For them, underdevelopment is "seen as extreme poverty and the almost total absence of growth. The poorest countries are therefore the most underdeveloped, and within individual countries the poorest regions are the most underdeveloped."[13] This definition permits us to look at underdevelopment within a particular country.

As stated earlier, the dependency theory is in fact a paradigm with several tendencies. One of the important trends, Marxism, will be examined in order to illustrate the different tendency the Marxist definition of underdevelopment follows. Sacouman, a Marxist theorist using the centre and periphery theory to explain underdevelopment, defines underdevelopment as follows: "Underdevelopment ... is a structural product of the global process of capital accumulation as it expands or contracts within specified areas."[14]

There are several areas of emphasis within the centre and periphery theory. Marxists choose to emphasise the "dynamics of the capitalist-working class, capitalist-petty producer, and capitalist-semi-proletarian relations of production."[15] For example, when these theorists discuss the Maritimes, they define the underdevelopment of certain areas with the existence of the following set of interrelated structural features:

> ... dependence within regions on primary production, the products of which are often exported to the capital centres for further processing; the creation and maintenance of large pools of cheap, surplus labour power, to be utilised, like any other commodity, as export material when demanded; and the export of surplus value to the capital centres. [16]

Within these trends found in the paradigm of dependency, particular notions also emerge. For example, Dos Santos developed three stages of dependency. The chronological division of these stages was reported in Magnus Blomstrom and Bjorn Hettne's book *Development Theory in Transition*. Dos Santos explains that the first state of dependency is "colonial dependence," the second "financial-industrial dependence," and the third "technological-industrial dependence."[17] Colonial dependence took place before the nineteenth century and was characterised by "colonial monopolies of land." The second stage of dependence took place in the nineteenth and early twentieth centuries. It is during this stage of financial-industrial dependence that the South was attributed with the role of exporter of raw materials. The final state of technological-industrial dependence took place after World War II. This third state is characterised by the creation of multinational corporations in the peripheral countries. Dos Santos calls this the "new dependence."

This concludes the first section of this chapter. The emergence of the dependency theory was described, and a list of theorists was provided. Dependency and underdevelopment were found to share a direct relationship. Self-reliance and wealth were key indicators when establishing the level of underdevelopment and dependency.

The following section will describe the importance of examining the internal as well as the external structures in a country. Historical, economic, and political dependence, as well as the relationship of control between the North and the South, will also be examined.

The Forms of Dependency

The centre and periphery theory states that, in general, the reason that one region is developed is because another is underdeveloped. James Sacouman states that "regionally uneven capitalist development at the short-end of the stick has always and everywhere meant underdevelopment."[18] Before this theory became popular in the late 1960s, theorists were concluding that the reason some regions were underdeveloped was because of the psychological state of their inhabitants. For example, in Canada, the stereotype of the Maritimer was examined in order to explain this region's underdevelopment. The typical Maritimer was said to "lack entrepreneurial drive, to account for the economy's relative lack of growth in the twentieth century; social-cultural backwardness, to account for rural poverty; and popular political conservatism, to blame the failure of social democracy in the region on the inherently tradition-bound Maritimer."[19] However, the Maritime provinces are now considered a peripheral region of Canada, and their inhabitants are no longer accused of "backwardness." First Nations Citizens have also been accused of laziness and "backwardness." It would follow, therefore, that dependency does not only exist between countries but also takes place within countries amongst regions. Each country has a region that is dependent on another, and in most cases the large urban centres dominate the rural areas. "Eduardo Galeano talks about a division of labour between and within nations whereby some specialise in winning and others in losing. Each country, he says, and each region of a given country, can be seen as an endless chain of dependency that has been endlessly extended. The chain has many more than two links."[20]

One of the key elements of the dependency theory is that the world is seen as one system. There are several dependency relationships that occur within specific countries amongst regions, but when discussing countries it is important to remember that they are a part of a world system. Samir Amin describes this relationship in his book entitled, *Accumulation on a World Scale*:

> Capitalism has become a world system, and not just a juxtaposition of "national capitalism." The social contradictions characteristic of capitalism are thus on a world scale, that is, the contradiction is not between the bourgeoisie and the proletariat of each country considered in isolation, but between the world bourgeoisie and the world proletariat.[21]

It has been established that central and peripheral countries are evolving in a world system, but which has more influence over the development of a country, internal or external structures? Roxborough distinguishes external dependency or "dependency as a relationship" by emphasising that the dependency is between two systems with clear boundaries. Here the dependency is created by the interchanges between the North and the South. However, internal dependency is predominant for many regions. This is caused when dependency is viewed "as a conditioning factor which alters the internal functioning and articulation of the elements of the dependent social formation."[22] Roxborough explains that a clear distinction lies between these two lines of thought: "the internal dynamics of the dependent social formation are fundamentally different from the internal dynamics of the social formations of advanced capitalism."[23] Some describe the dependency as purely economical, for this dependency is synonymous with lack of autonomy. Other dependency theorists are critical of this approach because it fails to look at the relationships between the classes, which in fact form and maintain the structures that create the dependency. Marxists believe that structures are controlled by the bourgeoisie, and these structures are responsible for the distribution and redistribution of commodities.

Social evolutionists believe in endogenous factors alone, while some dependency theorists are at the opposite end of the scale. They believe that all change in peripheral countries is caused by exogenous factors and that there are no elements within these regions that would create any change; all change is created by the outside. Taken independently, these two extremes have obvious limitations. Although it may be difficult to construct, the most appropriate theory is one which considers both endogenous and exogenous factors for the occurring changes.

An examination of internal structures is as important as the study of external structures, which is evident when examining the political situation of the dependent countries or regions.

Allahar points out the importance of examining the internal structures within dependent countries. The state of dependence is perpetuated, for one reason, "because political leaders in the dependent countries are generally reduced to being mere pawns of international capitalism."[24] They realize that their class interests are best met when they are cooperating with the centre.

When examining the internal political structures, one can understand how dominant countries still have a hold over peripheral countries or regions. Currently, when most countries have become "independent" of their "mother countries," the centre still controls the peripheral regions. It does this by controlling the political leaders of the periphery, who hold what Edward Herman and Noam Chomsky call "demonstration elections." The centre creates "client states with puppet governments whose financial and military strings are pulled in Washington or London."²⁵

Roxborough explains that the relationship that exists between the North and South has always been controlled by the North. The centre has changed the relationships with peripheral countries several times throughout history, to suit its needs. "Therefore, a first step in any analysis must be a periodisation of the stages of development of the centre. Only then can a typology of Third World countries be added to the schema."²⁶ Roxborough states that once the classes have been examined in a particular country, it is important to determine the nature of the relationships with the political structures. He points out that there does not exist a general theory which can be applied to all peripheral regions, but in fact these relationships are determined by examining the historical events of each region separately.

It is important to understand the emergence of the peripheral regions, and this can be found in a common history of imperialism and colonialism. However, one should not assume that social evolutionism will someday eliminate all peripheral regions. The first assumption made by evolutionists is that all Third World countries are or were feudal. Although there may be some resemblance to the feudal system, most of the structures are very different and, therefore, the external and internal conflicts are very disparate. Second, these regions began changing once they came into contact with the West, which was already changing at a rapid rate, and the periphery has been changing ever since that contact. Third, one cannot assume that the same evolution will take place for the simple reason that there is a lack of wealth and resources. If one considers the ancient civilisations of India and Latin America, these regions once had wealth, but this wealth disappeared after the West's expansion. Finally, diffusion takes place in these regions, whereby one society changes as a result of contact with another. These regions are expected to make the transition centuries after having been introduced into the world system as peripheral countries.

In order to truly understand a country's situation, one must examine all three structures: the political, the historical, and the socio-economic. When taking a closer look at the socio-economic structures, one will inevitably discuss the emergence of classes and of class conflicts.

Pablo Gonzalez Casanova and Harold Wolpe discuss the importance of examining the colonialist and imperialist hold over particular countries when studying their dependency:

> Those structures, both historical and contemporary, include such things as slavery, and the pattern of race relations that emerged, the monocrop plantation economy with the emphasis on the wholesale export of raw or semifinished products, foreign multinational corporations, and branch plant industries that drain the wealth and resources of the peripheral countries back to the metropolis, and the political arrangements that favour the (class) interests of those who are in control of such corporations.[27]

They continue by saying that when multinational corporations (MNCs) enter into the peripheral economic system, underdevelopment, rather than development, is promoted.

The most common way for the North to maintain the South's dependency is by establishing multinationals there. Allahar explains that "acting through their respective MNCs, the various fractions of the international commercial, manufacturing, industrial, and financial bourgeoisie come to yield a great deal of power in the countries of the periphery."[28] Many believed that development could take place by setting in motion the MNCs in the peripheral regions, but in fact this had the reverse effect. Allahar explains that the MNCs "denationalised" the economy, hence increasing "social inequalities." Allahar describes this process as follows:

> The constant draining away of national wealth, the monopolisation of the best lands by foreign corporations, the recruitment of trained experts from abroad, and the underdevelopment locally of health or educational facilities all accentuate social and economic disparities between the mass of the workers and peasants, and the tiny core of privileged classes that benefit from the imperialist connection.[29]

When using the centre and periphery theory, it is important to understand how these regions were formed. Ian Roxborough argues that these regions were created when societies changed from feudalism to capitalism. There were three major changes that took place with this transition: the conflicts between the landowners and the peasants, urbanisation, and the evolution of a centralised state. Roxborough continues by explaining that for this chain of events to take place there had to be a rapid increase in capital. Two methods were employed to increase capital, "the first was colonial blunder; the sacking of the wealth of the peripheral areas of the world."[30] The second was the confiscation of the land held by peasants and the church. These methods of "freeing" capital also created a landless class.

Samir Amin argues that capitalism was spread in the peripheral countries by creating a "merchant" capitalist class. This was a relatively small class that exported materials to the merchant classes in the centre. The profits went to a small percentage of the peripheral population. Furthermore, this merchant class did not ensure any kind of distribution, nor did it set up appropriate social structures.

The notion of class is important to most dependency theorists. They argue that there is a large difference between the classes of the centre and the classes found in the periphery. A large part of the differences between the classes is that those found in the periphery are more complex and much weaker. Their weakness and complexity comes from the fact that their ruling classes are incomplete, a large part of them being found in countries of the centre. Quite often the battles that occur between classes are in fact between citizens of more than one country. For example, workers who are citizens of peripheral countries are in direct conflict with multinational corporations that are owned by citizens of a country in the centre. This concept reflects Samir Amin's notion of a single world structure, although Roxborough prefers to consider only the ruling class as one belonging to this world system, and he believes that all other classes are formed at a national level. Another reason for the complexity of the class structures in peripheral countries is the fact that there are two internal struggles within these countries: the conflict between the bourgeoisie and the proletariat and the struggle for the countries' release from the external hold. Citizens are fighting to stop the process of dependency and, at the same time, fighting among themselves. These conflicts are separate and yet related, and their importance depends on the country. The conflicts are interwoven, and they contribute to the complexity of the structures of the classes in the periphery.

In Marxist terms, the periphery furnishes cheap labour and raw materials for the centre. In the past, the centre would take hold of these resources by conquering these territories. Establishing themselves as mother countries, they assured themselves an endless supply. "In this way the politically and economically powerful classes in the mother countries benefited at the expense largely of the indigenous inhabitants of the colonies."[31]

The peripheral countries or regions are primarily viewed as exporters of raw materials. Whether these products are agricultural or mineral, these regions are stripped so that others benefit. The raw materials are exported to where they are processed into finished products. They are then returned to their point of origin with an inflated price tag. The profits are not inherent in the raw materials but are found in the finished products. Thus, capital is accumulated in the centre. The centre not only benefits from the profits, but also from the jobs that are created by the manufacturing industry. The workers of the centre are employed and, therefore, have more money to spend, hence creating a service industry. Allahar states that dependency theorists see this economic "rape" of a country's wealth as directly related to its continued dependence and backwardness.[32] The peripheral regions become dependent because they neglect their internal markets, since all of their structures are developed for exportation. Part of their dependence stems from the fact that they have tailored "their economies to meet the needs of the advanced ones."[33]

In summary, it is important to examine internal as well as external structures, while acknowledging the possible dominance of outside powers by political means. It is also important to study the emergence of peripheral regions. Historical studies clarify the creation of classes and the division of labour. Finally, peripheral regions were once and still are mere exporters of raw materials to the centres, and most of them are still underdeveloped, regardless of their industrialisation.

Applying the Dependency Theory in Canada

This section will put forward an example by Kari Levitt and Jorge Niosi, who applied the dependency theory to Canada. Levitt and Niosi conclude that Canada is in fact the "world's richest underdeveloped country." As stated in the previous section, Allahar sees a direct relationship between underdevelopment and the presence of multinational corporations (MNCs).

Levitt and Niosi both describe the role of foreign capital in Canada by outlining how American companies establish branch plants in Canada that only serve to drain capital out of the country. Jorge Niosi describes the process of control with regard to Canadian technology: "Canada, after a century of pursuing a liberal policy towards foreign direct investment and the transfer of technology, now finds itself (although this has begun to change) with half of its technology under outside control — one of the highest percentages of foreign control in the world."[34]

Wallace Clement, Ralph Matthews, and Henry Veltmeyer were a few of the theorists who used the dependency theory to explain regional differences within Canada. They all agreed that Canada's dependency stemmed from its historical background, when it was dependent on its mother country, and whereby its political and economic structures became British. They claim that as Canada began to detach itself from Britain and began trading more with its neighbour, Canada became more dependent on the United States. Hence, because of this increase in dependence, the regional disparities were accentuated. Clement believes this occurred because the "regional economies are tied to national economies and national ones to international ones," thus creating a chain.[35]

As discussed earlier, the South had the raw materials and the North had the industries to create the final products. Because of this division, the North was the only one to profit from the raw resources. The South lost the employment created by manufacturing, lost profits, and neglected to develop their internal trading structures. Clement found that because Canada was divided into an industrial sector and a hinterland, this process occurred in Canada as well. Industrial Canada can be found between Windsor and Montréal. Even though there are other industrial pockets across the country, there are some regions that are clearly "underdeveloped," for example, the Atlantic provinces and the northern parts of the country. These regions have wealth, but it is a wealth made up of natural resources and not financial institutions or production plants. Therefore, the wages and employment rates remain low in these regions whose only source of income is from raw materials. Matthews describes the consequences of this underdevelopment: "social development is neglected; schools, hospitals, and housing are substandard; and the general life chances of the population are not as promising as those of Canadians who live, for example, in the 'golden triangle' (Toronto-Montréal-Ottawa)."[36] A typical example of a periphery is a single industry town, where the population is entirely dependent on the operation of this industry, and not one job would be spared if this one industry closed its doors.

If the starting point to underdevelopment in Canada is colonialism, then one may ask how Canada is different from other countries that were colonized, for example, in Africa and in Latin America. Allahar attributes the difference to the fact that Canada, Australia, and New Zealand were colonized differently. They were not simply stripped of their resources; the colonizers wanted to establish themselves in their colonies. They were interested in "homesteading and farming." They saw these territories as a future home, not just as a source of raw materials.

Canada is an underdeveloped country according to many dependency theorists, but it is an exception along with Australia and New Zealand. Even though Canada depends on external funds and technology, making it underdeveloped, it is not underdeveloped like the countries of the South. The standard of living and the economic, social, and political structures make Canada different. The reason for this, as stated previously, is that Canada, Australia, and New Zealand were marked as "settling" colonies, not areas to be used simply to extract raw materials. The important point to remember, however, is that there are elements that create dependency: political, economic, social, and technological factors. It is also important to remember that there are underdeveloped regions within

Canada. The question that remains to be studied is whether the Cree nation is underdeveloped.

Dependency theorists recognise that dependency and underdevelopment are directly related, and, furthermore, that underdevelopment is fatal for the dependent region. The question most asked when studying a theory is the end result: What does this theory propose as a solution to this problem?

One of the two solutions to the existence of the centre and periphery, according to Roxborough, is revolution, seen as an alternative to dependency. Change is needed in order to stop the dependency, but these "much-needed reforms are impossible without a restructuring of the mode of articulation of the economy with the world economy."[37] However, many dependency theorists agree that revolutions would be impossible because they would be opposed by the upper-class in the periphery and by all members of the centre; hence, revolution is the one solution to be considered at a later time.

However, there are other theorists like Samir Amin who believe in something other than revolution. Amin believes in delinking, which, in fact, means self-reliance. This solution does not mean complete detachment from the centre. It only means control by the periphery over their political, social, and economic structures. Delinking is recommended by Samir Amin as a possible solution to the international problem of Third World countries. Delinking is not a complete cut from the central economic system, but it is an "awareness" of self-development. Samir Amin explains that "the meaning is as follows: pursuit of a system of rational criteria for economic options founded on law of value on a national basis with popular relevance, independent of such criteria of economic rationality as flow from the dominance of the capitalist law of value operating on a world scale."[38] Delinking does not mean a complete break from the centre, and Samir Amin acknowledges that this is impossible for Third World countries. However, the periphery must seize the chance of becoming more autonomous whenever the opportunity presents itself. A Third World country can only gain autonomy through self-development, as opposed to development for the centre. The economic decisions that are to be made must come from the people of the periphery and not the economists in the centre. The economic decisions must make sense and improve the survival of the people in these underdeveloped regions.

As mentioned earlier, delinking does not mean a complete alienation from the centre; however, it means an awareness of one's needs. By gaining control over their political, social, and economic situation, the peripheries will, over time, gain self-sufficiency. There still is contact that would exist between underdeveloped countries and the centre, but trade would eventually be more fair. For example, technology is something that cannot be exchanged on an equal level, but Samir Amin indicates the healthy attitude that peripheries must acquire:

> Delinking does not imply rejection of all foreign technology, simply for being foreign, in the name of some culturalist nationalism. But it certainly does imply an awareness that technology is not neutral, either in terms of social relations of production, or in terms of models of living and consumption, priority given to the involvement of the whole country, the entire people, in the process of change dictates a mix of modern technologies (possibly imported) and renovation and improvement of traditional technologies.[39]

The possibilities of applying these two solutions to the Cree of James Bay will be examined in the conclusion of this book. A choice between revolution and delinking is what the dependency theory suggests.

The dependency theory is in fact part of a paradigm. For the purpose of this discussion, the difference between underdeveloped and undeveloped regions will be considered, as well as the internal and external factors that influence the degree of dependency. The following chapters will apply this theory to the Cree of James Bay, in an attempt to treat the Cree as an underdeveloped nation within a nation. The next chapter will examine the emergence of the Cree as a periphery throughout history.

Notes

1. Allahar, Anton L. *Sociology and the Periphery: Theories and Issues*. Garamond Press, Toronto, 1989, p.90.
2. Roxborough, Ian. *Theories of Underdevelopment*. The Macmillan Press Ltd., London, 1983, p.42.
3. Ibid., p.43.
4. Ibid., p.66.
5. Dos Santos, in Allahar, Anton L. *Sociology and the Periphery: Theories and Issues*, p.89.
6. Hall, Thomas D. "Is Historical Sociology of Peripheral Regions eripheral?" *Studies in Political Economy a Socialist Review: Rethinking Canadian Political Economy*. no.6, Autumn 1981, p.351.
7. Allahar, Anton L. *Sociology and the Periphery: Theories and Issues*, p.82.
8. Ibid., p.85.
9. Bromley, D.F. Rosemary, and Ray Bromley. *South American Development: A Geographical Introduction*. Cambridge University Press, Cambridge, 1988, p.15.
10. Ibid., p.16.
11. Allahar, Anton L. *Sociology and the Periphery: Theories and Issues*, p.85.
12. Bromley, D.F. Rosemary, and Ray Bromley. *South American Development: A Geographical Introduction*, p.6.
13. Ibid., p.13.
14. Sacouman, James R. "The 'Peripheral' Maritimes and Canada-Wide Marxist Political Economy." *Studies in Political Economy a Socialist Review: Rethinking Canadian Political Economy*. no.6, Autumn 1981:135-51, p.142.
15. Ibid., p.140.
16. Ibid., p.142.
17. Blomstrom, Magnus and Bjorn Hettne. *Development Theory in Transition: The Dependency Debate and Beyond: Third World Responses*, Zed Books Ltd., London, 1984, p.65.
18. Sacouman, James R. "The 'Peripheral' Maritimes and Canada-Wide Marxist Political Economy." *Studies in Political Economy: A Socialist Review: Rethinking Canadian Political Economy*, p.135.
19. Ibid., p.136.

20. Allahar, Anton L. *Sociology and the Periphery: Theories and Issues*, p.86.
21. Roxborough, Ian. *Theories of Underdevelopment*, p.47.
22. Ibid., p.44.
23. Ibid.
24. Allahar, Anton L. *Sociology and the Periphery: Theories and Issues*, p.90-91.
25. Ibid., p.92.
26. Roxborough, Ian. *Theories of Underdevelopment*, p.53.
27. Allahar, Anton L. *Sociology and the Periphery: Theories and Issues*, p.86.
28. Ibid., p.93.
29. Ibid., p.95.
30. Roxborough, Ian. *Theories of Underdevelopment*, p.10.
31. Allahar, Anton L. *Sociology and the Periphery: Theories and Issues*, p.92.
32. Ibid., p.90.
33. Ibid.
34. Niosi, in Allahor, op. cit., p.97.
35. Ibid., p.98.
36. Ibid., p.99.
37. Roxborough, Ian. *Theories of Underdevelopment*, p.69.
38. Amin, Samir. *La faillite du développement en Afrique et dans le Tiers-Monde*. L'-Harmattan, Paris, 1989, p.2.
39. Ibid., p.4.

Chapter 2

Becoming a Periphery:
The James Bay Cree from 1600-1920

Using the dependency theory described in chapter one, this chapter will examine the emergence of the James Bay area as a periphery and its residents, the Cree, as dependents. As previously stressed, it is important to understand the emergence of a particular periphery. Roxborough identified a general theory that can be applied to all peripheral regions, but these relationships are determined by examining the historical events of each region separately. The emergence of peripheral regions can be found in a common history of imperialism and colonialism, but one should not assume that social evolutionism will someday eliminate all peripheral regions. This chapter will examine the history of the James Bay Cree in relationship to the history of imperialism and colonialism.

The core of industrial Canada can be found between Windsor and Montréal. Even though there are other industrial pockets throughout the country, there are some regions that are clearly "underdeveloped": the Atlantic Provinces and the northern parts of the country. These regions have wealth, but it is a wealth made up of natural resources and not financial institutions or production plants. Therefore, the wages and employment rates remain low in these regions, whose only source of income is from raw materials. This chapter will begin with the basic assumption that James Bay, being a part of Canada's north, is a peripheral area. It will discuss how this region became an area whose only source of income is from raw materials, and how it is controlled by the centre.

As mentioned in the discussion of dependency, Allahar attributes the difference between, on the one hand, colonized countries like Canada, Australia, and New Zealand and, on the other hand, countries of the Third World, to the different way in which colonization took place. He argues that they were not simply stripped of their resources, but the colonizers wanted to establish themselves in their colonies. They were interested in "homesteading and farming." They saw these territories as future homes, not as pure resources. It will be demonstrated that the colonizers had no intention of settling in northern areas and, hence, stripped these regions of their natural resources.

The first chapter of this book described Dos Santos' three stages of dependency. The first, "colonial dependence," took place before the nineteenth century and was characterised by "colonial monopolies of land." In "financial-industrial dependence," the second stage, the role of exporter of raw materials was attributed to the North, and took place in the nineteenth and early twentieth century. The final stage is "technological-industrial dependence," which took place after World War II. This third stage, which will be discussed in the next two chapters, was characterised by the creation of multi-national corporations in peripheral countries. Dos Santos calls this the "new dependence."

This chapter will be divided into two sections: the first will describe the James Bay Cree before the arrival of the colonizers, and the second section will combine Dos Santos' first and second stages of dependency, based on events that took place between 1600-1920. These dates where chosen because they cover the arrival of the Hudson's Bay Company (HBC) and "to all intents and purposes the [HBC] was left in effective control of [this] region until the end of World War I."[1] This chapter is descriptive in nature, examining the major changes that were imposed on the Cree in those 320 years. The following chapter will combine the remaining seventy years in an analysis of the political and socio-economic dependence of the Cree.

Pre-Encounter

As previously quoted, Allahar asserts that all theorists agree that underdevelopment "is not the original state or stage in which all countries once found themselves."[2] Dependency theorists believe that underdevelopment is a state that came after contact with imperialist nations. These peripheral regions began changing once they came into contact with colonizers, who were already changing at a rapid rate, and the periphery has been changing in response to colonizers ever since. This section is a brief description of the life of the Cree before they encountered their colonizers. There are two parts to this section: the first will describe the physical and general facts regarding the Cree, and the second will describe their social organisation. All aspects of their lives, including social organisation, religion, housing, and nutrition, will be covered.

The origin of the Natives on this continent dates back 12,000 and 30,000 years ago.[3] Since archaeologists have not found any fossils from the pre-modern area, they maintain that the Natives crossed the then frozen Bering Strait from Asia to the Eastern Hemisphere. "By the sixteenth century, an estimated 350,000 Natives roamed most of Canada's landmass."[4]

Some may find it confusing that there is a nation called the Lubicon Cree in western Canada, but this is because the Crees were spread out across the northern part of Canada and inhabited areas from western Québec all the way to British Columbia. Because of this great distance, many of the bands developed their own dialects. The Cree and the Montagnais languages are very similar, while the Ojibwa and Algonkin are more closely related. "Linguists working in James Bay today are in agreement that all Indians of the Québec-Labrador peninsula speak the same language, Montagnais, which they divide into three major dialects."[5]

Available sources do not report the names and areas occupied by bands in James Bay before the seventeenth century.

Although the primary focus in this section is the sixteenth century, French records dating from the first half of the seventeenth century reported that there were "four groups that are now regarded as Cree: the Mistassins in the Mistassini Lake area, the Escurieux along the Prince Rupert, the Nisibourounik to the west of the mouths of the Nottaway and Rupert rivers on James Bay, and the Pitchibarenik near the mouth of the Eastmain River."[6] Francis and Morantz report that the early name of the Cree was "Kilistinins." They also report that in 1660 an Indian traveller mentioned that there were in fact nine bands of Cree that inhabited the James Bay area. For the purposes of this discussion, the Cree will be identified by the forts or lakes by which they live, since all old and recent sources do not distinguish these bands by name. Moreover, "the name[s] disappear[ed] from the records as the English speak only of 'Indians'."[7] The first map in the appendix provides a clear picture of where these lakes and forts are located.

A specialist, Kenneth Hare, described the vegetation in the James Bay and the Ungava and Labrador peninsula. He distinguished four basic types of vegetation. The first is located north of fifty-nine degrees latitude, about 350 miles north of Fort George. The Tundra is a treeless region, where vegetation is limited to small shrubs, lichens, and mosses. The second region, located between fifty-nine and fifty-five degrees latitude, is called the forest tundra. The vegetation between the Great Whale River and north of Fort George is still treeless, as in the first area, but it has small scattered pockets of trees located in the low grounds. The third area, north of Rupert House and south of Eastmain, is composed of forest land, where there are trees scattered all over the area with mosses and lichens covering the land in between. The vegetation south of fifty-two degrees latitude is described as a forest area where the sunlight does not reach the ground.[8]

The Cree in James Bay hunted many animals throughout the year, but they had an annual distinctive pattern. Every September and October they would hunt the Canada Geese and other birds that stopped in their feeding grounds on their way south. The Cree would then return to their settlement in October to prepare their journey to their trapline. They would remain on their trapline until March, hunting beaver and large game. After having returned to their settlement, they would prepare to meet the birds on their migration north, and they would hunt until the end of May. The Crees would then return to their settlement and fish during the months of July and August, when it would be time to prepare for the trek to rendez-vous with the Canada geese. The cycle continued in this way. This example is from the Rupert House Cree, but there were some variances among the bands depending on their geographic location. All bands, without exception, had cycles whereby all would go to their trapline between October and March, when they would hunt beaver and large game, and all would fish during the summer months.[9]

Francis and Morantz describe the social organisation of the James Bay Cree by centring their description on the local group. The local group was composed of one Cree heading a group of six to nine hunters and their families. The traplines of these hunters were located near the settlement of the local group. The average family size was five individuals, and the local groups varied in size between thirty and fifty people. When time came to go to their traplines, the local group would divide into smaller groups composed of two to three families, and hunting groups varied between ten to fifteen men, women, and children. The hunting group would build teepees as shelters for the winter, with one teepee housing the entire hunting group. These were made of canvas and four long wooden poles. The ground would be covered by moss gathered by the women, and there would be a "chimney" to let the fire smoke blow outside. Women and children were responsible for the cooking, for collecting firewood, and for checking the traps set near the camp. Men often left the camp all day or overnight when in search of large game. "The territories averaged approximately 712.4 square miles. They ranged in size from approximately 225 square miles to approximately 3,000 square miles."[10] The concept of land ownership was quite different from the European definition. There were the notions of longevity, occupancy, and heredity, but the central theme was the animals. If there were no animals, they would not claim the land. Yet the meat from the animals in these territories was shared by all. The boundaries were defined so that the resources would not be depleted due to the presence of several hunting groups in the territories. The boundaries of the traplines were also there as a safety measure and as a warning to other Crees about trap locations. There were no maps, yet every hunter would be well aware of the traplines surrounding his own.

For each hunting camp there was a leader, who would most likely be the owner of the trapline. This position was one of "prestige," but it was also associated with religion. Adrian Tanner describes the leader as follows: "He [could not] openly show authority. But at the religious and judicial level, he exercise[d] power over animals and ha[d] a property relationship with the land by the group."[11] One of the religious duties of the leader was to conduct ceremonies, for example, rights of passage and praying to the animals. The leader had to thank the animals for allowing themselves to get caught, hence demonstrating respect for the animals.

Tanner associates the Cree religion with the productivity of the group. On one hand, a hunter reached his peak of productivity in his twenties and thirties, but, on the other hand, religious maturity was possessed by elders. Since each camp required both the hunter and the religious figure, the productivity level of the young men would be equated with that of the old men, therefore providing a logical reason for the equal distribution of food.

There were several ways that a hunter could relinquish his trapline to a younger hunter. The first and most obvious was for the hunter to present his land to his son, son-in-law, or other kin.

But a hunter who was about to retire may have handed his trapline over to a fellow hunter who perhaps had been a guest hunter on his trapline several times before. Another option was to relinquish the land to an individual member of an adjacent trapline.

In summary, the general life that the James Bay Cree lead before the "encounter," was one of self-sufficiency. There were some years when animals were scarce, and in these years a few Crees would die of starvation. However, one must consider the life in Europe in the sixteenth century and prior to it in order to put these few deaths into perspective. During and before the sixteenth century, the Cree were self-sustaining and were dependent on no one, for food, for decisions, or for credit. The following section will describe the first 320 years when Europeans and the Crees co-inhabited the same "province." The conclusion will stress the differences between these two eras, showing the consequent emergence of the north as a peripheral region dependent on the centre.

When Whites Met Natives

The following section will examine the events that took place after Europeans arrived in Canada. Denys Delâge makes an interesting point in his book, *Le Pays Renversé*, where he writes about the history of the three colonial empires: Holland, England, and France. This brief history explains how each country became a colonizer in a different way and for different reasons. Delâge states that during the first half of the seventeenth century Holland was the centre in Europe, while England and then France were the semi-core and Spain and Portugal were the semi-peripheral regions. Holland had a large fleet and shipyards, with which they controlled the North Sea and the British Isles fishing coast. During the sixteenth century, they were the largest suppliers of fish to England. Because of this power, Holland was able to push the English and the French south to Newfoundland and to take over the Labrador coast for their fishing. The English were the first to have a settlement on Newfoundland, mainly due to their need for salt to keep the fish from wasting. Because they had to import the salt at a great cost, they developed other storing methods for which they needed installations. The French and the Spaniards had the salt and would fish and immediately sail back to their countries with the fish nicely stored. The English naval force, being greater than that of the French, pushed the French deep into the St. Lawrence where they discovered something they had not started off looking for: the "fur trade." They began their trade in Nova Scotia and then at Tadoussac, but it was not until 1605 that they established their first trading post in the Bay of Fundy. Once again, the English pushed the French further along the St. Lawrence river, where they began building Québec City in 1608. Holland, interested in France's new business, bought royalties in the French companies. Holland sent an Englishman, Henry Hudson, to explore what it now known as the Hudson river. Holland thrived because it had the fastest boats and controlled the fish markets of Europe. The important point to note, however, was that the Dutch did not immigrate to Canada, because of their good economic position in Europe. They were the "core" and had religious tolerance and a prosperous agriculture. The English immigrated in large numbers due to several problems in their country. For example, farmers were having their land taken away, so they immigrated where there was free land. The French also immigrated to the new country because they were overpopulated. This overview of European countries in the sixteenth century helps to explain the pockets of settlements that grew from the international situation at the time.[12]

As noted above, Henry Hudson sailed his ship, the "Discovery," up the Hudson river in 1611, where the first recorded encounter between a white man and a James Bay Cree took place. Because the Hudson Bay was not a passage to the Far East, however, this region was ignored. There were only a few Europeans who entered the region without settling. They found that the Cree already knew about trading, that in fact they had been trading with Europeans at the mouth of the Saguenay at Tadoussac, with the Montagnais acting as middle men. Radisson and Des Groseilliers were the first to look for backing to exploit the fur trade in the James Bay area. Although they were two Frenchmen, they found their backing from English merchants. They named the Rupert River after the king's cousin, Prince Rupert, who later became the first governor of the Hudson's Bay Company.

The Hudson's Bay Company's first post was Rupert House, which was established in 1668. In the spring of 1669, the pelts of 300 Cree hunters were brought back to London. At this point, the fruitfulness of the Hudson Bay was confirmed, and in May 1670 "the English king granted to a group of English merchants and aristocrats calling itself the Hudson's Bay Company exclusive trading rights in the approximately 3 million square miles of North America draining into the great bay."[13] The rate of development in the area can be seen in the number of fort constructions in a decade. Charles Fort, although built in 1670, was not occupied year-round until 1672. On the Moose River, Moose Fort was built in 1673, and on the Albany River, a fort bearing the same name was established in 1679.

In the first chapter of this book, Dos Santos' dependency was described as follows: "a situation in which a certain group of countries have their economies conditioned by the development and expansion of another economy, to which their own is subjected."[14] Now that the evolution of the HBC has been outlined, a discussion of the unequal trade that took place between the HBC and the Cree will be examined. Denys Delâge states the consequences of an unequal exchange between the Cree and the Europeans:

> *Le développement du commerce des fourrures intègre rapidement les Amérindiens dans une économie de marché. A partir de ce moment, ils sont prisonniers d'une mécanique implacable qui les conduira a leur appauvrissement et à leur dépendence, tandis que leur travail permettra aux marchands de se constituer des fortunes et de mettre sur pied une machine militaire qui se retournera contre eux.*[15]

Delâge states that the unequal exchange led to dependency and poverty for the Cree, and wealth and power for the Europeans. Delâge explains that not all exchange is unequal; it becomes unequal when it takes place between a "modern" society and a "primitive" society. Accumulation is what leads to an unequal exchange, when one party is seeking profit. Unequal exchange is also present when the productivity levels are different. For example, it took much longer for a Native to obtain a beaver pelt than it took for Europeans to produce some flour. Delâge ends this section of his book by offering a list of the principle implications for Natives with respect to unequal exchange. Delâge notes nine effects of unequal exchange, translated and summarised as follows: (1) Trade could not take place in a compatible form because the fur trade took place between one economy that was based on the accumulation of capital and another based on a "primitive" economy. (2) As trade progressed, bonds were created between the communities, and the "primitive" trader learned of the real prices of his merchandise, and, therefore, became less willing to accept the Europeans' low prices. (3) The new economic system brought about new divisions of labour, bringing specialisation as well as a hierarchical system between and within bands. (4) As trading progressed, there developed a larger diversity of supplies from Europe which were traded, hence there was a dependence created for these supplies. (5) These once independent regions slowly became the peripheral regions of the centre, Europe. (6) The periphery recognised that their productive systems were not as "productive" as those of the centre, hence the peripheral areas were always trying to possess the "modern" techniques of production. (7) Natural resources were depleted because the periphery always needed to produce more in order to receive the products produced in the centre. (8) The natural resources become more valuable to members of the periphery, multiplying the wars between the peoples of the periphery. (9) As the wealth of Europe grew and as the poverty of the Natives increased, the centre feared attacks from the periphery, hence the need for armies.[16]

Francis and Morantz argue, on the other hand, that there was no unequal trade in James Bay. They argue that each trading post had a list of trade "prices" that were issued by the HBC, which listed everything from a blanket, for six beaver pelts, to a four foot gun, worth twelve beaver pelts. Other examples of these "prices" include the following: one yard of cloth was worth two beaver pelts; two beaver pelts could also be traded for a "plain" hat; and one gallon of brandy could be received in exchange for four pelts of beaver.[17] These "prices" were quite steep, considering the average hunter would have twenty pelts to trade per season. Even though these prices were fixed by the HBC, the company representatives said that they tried to trade for as little as the Cree would accept. If they became aware of this list, the trade masters were even reported "cheating the scale" so that Natives thought they were getting more. The HBC trade masters describe the Natives as unwilling to accept any change, so that when the HBC wanted to give better deals to the Natives to meet the prices of the competition, the Natives were reported unwilling to accept these price changes, even if they were in their favour.

Francis and Morantz argue that there was no unequal trade; furthermore, that the Natives did not become dependent on the HBC. They maintain that there was a mutual dependency, whereby the Europeans needed the meat, snowshoes, canoes, and sleds as much as the hunters needed flour and guns.

The preceding discussion outlines the economy of the Natives as conditioned by outside sources. Europeans introduced the Cree into a capitalist world economy when they were not even at a feudal stage, even if this was not the direction in which they were necessarily heading. Once in this world economy, the Natives were "swallowed" up and forced to take on the role of a periphery sustaining the core.

Samir Amin argues that capitalism was spread in the peripheral countries by creating a "merchant" capitalist class. This was a relatively small class that exported materials to the merchant classes in the centre, with profits going to a small percentage of the peripheral population. Furthermore, this merchant class did not ensure any kind of distribution, nor did they set up appropriate social structures. As stated previously, a major difference between the classes is that those found in the periphery are more complex and much weaker, given that their ruling classes are incomplete, with a large part of them being found in countries of the centre.

The HBC created a "merchant" class similar to the one described by Samir Amin and others. In the late eighteenth century, postmasters appointed several "Indian lieutenants." These were Natives rewarded for bringing in hunters to a particular post for trading. These men were rewarded for spreading the trading system to their Native peoples. The lieutenants would receive gifts, such as "brandy, tobacco, and, to distinguish them as leaders, an outfit of quasi-military clothing."[18] They were given gifts in relation to the amount of pelts they would bring. The leaders were appointed for life, and each trading post had ten or twelve lieutenants, also called captains. The HBC chose leaders who had influence over "their people," enough influence to recruit hunters. Some shared the liquor they received with their hunters, but most of them formed a class of their own. They were middlemen who specialised in trading and who did not hunt. At the trading posts before the trading would commence, they performed small ceremonies with political undertones. And like the class which Samir Amin describes, they were fragile. Once the HBC decided that their leaders were too expensive, the "formal captaincy" was abolished.[19]

Whenever discussing the Third World, one always considers the national debt of each of the peripheral countries. The national debt plays a large role in determining the level of dependence of these countries. The HBC made the Natives dependent on particular trading posts by extending credit to them. This practice began in the first half of the eighteenth century. As the Natives would leave the posts in the fall, they would be given quantities of supplies for the bush which would be deducted from their spring furs. The amount of credit was determined by their previous season's catch. The HBC did this to keep the Natives trading with them instead of the inland competition. Most were given a credit of ten to twelve beaver pelts. The HBC found that they could manipulate the Natives into trading with them by giving them the credit, but they were always careful not to give too much so that the hunter would not move to the competition once his debt accumulated, or so that the hunter would not die with a large debt, which the company would lose. Decades later, the HBC introduced new regulations assigning Natives to a particular post so that they could not avoid paying their debts, thereby limiting the hunters' movements from that day onward. As Rolf Knight summarises, "in addition to a feeling of dependence by the local people, there is a very real dependence upon the credit allowed by the manager to individual trappers."[20]

Pablo Gonzalez Casanova and Harold Wolpe discuss the importance of examining the colonialist and imperialist hold over particular countries when studying the dependency of countries, such as the political arrangements which favour the financial institutions of the centre.[21] In 1828, the HBC began assigning not only trading posts as previously seen, but also assigning land to hunting families. This arrangement only benefitted the company and consequently rearranged the social organisation of the Natives. The HBC's division of land had little regard for the previous traplines or for non-monogamous families. In fact, as many as one-sixth of the families were polygamous at the time. The HBC redistributed the land to monogamous families, creating a number of dependent women and children who had been the second and third wives.

Many historical sources write about the beaver conservations that were set up by the HBC, once again ignoring the Native patterns of conservation. The hunters would let their trapline rest for a year or more, acting as a guest hunter on another man's trapline. This was done to replenish the land. These methods, however, were not good enough for the HBC, and so beaver conservations were introduced.

The HBC feared that the beaver would become extinct, so they introduced regulations that would discourage Natives from killing the cubs. The HBC banned steal traps, except in fox country. Moreover, they refused to trade any pelts that were attained in the summer months. There were economic reasons to this ban, since both the beaver cub pelts and the beavers killed in the summer season were not valuable to European traders. As mentioned previously, however, the trappers would not kill beavers in the summer and would "rotate" the use of their land. They did accept the HBC's new policies for the simple reason that they had always believed in these practices; not for economic reasons, but for their respect for the beaver. In 1827 the HBC, still afraid that Natives would kill beavers in the summer season, reduced the prices of the fishing supplies by one-third.[22]

The first beaver conservation site was on Charlton Island in 1836. Beavers were placed on the island, which was off-limits to all hunters. Two families resided on the island to make sure that there were no poachers or natural predators like the otter and lynx.[23] Limited hunting was allowed once the beaver population reached a certain number. James Bay's second conservation site was established in 1842 on Ministikawatin Island.

In 1841, the HBC introduced new restrictions on the trapping of beavers. This three year plan forbade Natives to trade more than one half of what they had traded in the 1838-39 season. "To offset this restriction the Indians were offered premiums for trapping marten instead of beaver."[24] Three years later, as promised, Natives were allowed to trap as many in-season beavers as they wished.

By the mid-eighteenth century, the HBC was offering full-time employment for "mixed bloods" and Natives. They would act as servants and supply men. However, the HBC soon found that there was a drawback in recruiting these reliable men, in that their families would become dependent on the post. The wives and children would set up camp outside the fort, but whenever they could not capture enough fish or small game to sustain themselves, they would become dependent on their husbands. Since their husbands worked for the posts, these women and children would become dependent on the company. The HBC implemented regulations in an attempt to limit the number of dependents. To begin, they forbade men to marry without the consent of the postmaster. In 1827, a man could not marry without leaving one-tenth of his earnings to the HBC, in case of his death or retirement. A decade later, a man could be fired if he refused the right of the Company to send his fifteen year old sons to distant posts as apprentices. Finally, in 1870, the HBC decided that these dependents were much too costly and opted to return to their practice of recruiting their servants from Europe.

James Bay Natives were controlled by political arrangements that primarily benefited the HBC. They were assigned land that was already organised, their family structures were altered, and their hunting habits were controlled for the economic benefit of the HBC. By assigning families to the land and trading posts, they were able to control the credit of each hunter. Moreover, by restricting the trapping of cub and summer beavers, they did not have to trade these "worthless" pelts for the "good" supplies. Finally, the HBC even sought to control the marriages of Natives at the posts, which would, once again, benefit them economically by creating fewer dependents for the post.

Allahar was quoted earlier as saying that part of the peripheries' dependence stems from the fact that they have tailored "their economies to meet the needs of the advanced ones."[25] In the examples mentioned above, it is clear that the James Bay Natives did tailor their economies. They altered their hunting patterns to suit the HBC, and many gave up hunting altogether to take up year-round employment with the company. Many others took seasonal employment with the HBC as "delivery" personnel.

This section would be incomplete if there was no mention of the competition of the HBC and its implications. Neither the English nor the HBC had competition from the French until 1682. Before then, only a few Natives would trust middlemen to trade their furs with the French in the south. The Compagnie du Nord was formed in 1682 by a group of merchants who "received a charter from the king of France enabling it to trade into Hudson Bay."[26] From then on the French and the English battled for the trade. They captured each other's forts and maintained a price war. The French in the south were complaining that the Natives were simply bringing their furs to the captured posts. Natives were reported to prefer trading with the French because they were more familiar with the land and better at surviving the winter, but ultimately the best trades, service, and treatment determined with whom the hunters would trade. The French diminished their presence in the James Bay area, although they did remain after 1713, "when according to the terms of the Treaty of Utrecht the French recognized the Hudson's Bay Company's claim to all of the bay."[27]

The conflict between the French and the English influenced Natives. For example, hunters of Eastmain House began complaining about "French" Indians. Francis and Morantz argue that this competition was good for the hunters because it allowed them to "manipulate" the trading prices. This is one of the points which is a part of their argument that the James Bay Natives were in no way dependent on the HBC, because they controlled the prices, and because they were trading their technology with the white technology as opposed to replacing the old with the new. However, the Compagnie du Nord was disorganised and did not pose a real threat to the English. In 1904, however, the Revillion Frère, a trading company established by a few Frenchmen, arrived in James Bay. Unlike the Compagnie du Nord, they were very organised. They established trading posts down river from the HBC, which allowed them to intercept the pelts before the English received them. This organised competition meant better goods, with a greater variety, and an increase in local wages for the James Bay Natives. Their reign ended when the great depression of the 1930s broke them, resulting in their holdings being officially transferred to the HBC in 1936.

Even though the impact of the education system and the influence of the Catholic and Protestant religions will not be discussed until the next chapter, a brief history of their first settlements follows.

The first schoolmaster arrived in the James Bay area in 1808. James Clouston was responsible for the education of whites and "mixed blood" children. At this point, the HBC recognised the usefulness of having clergymen posted in the area, to assimilate Natives. The missionary, George Barnley, arrived in James Bay in the mid-1840s. He and his wife were recalled to England after his attempts to introduce reading, writing, and religion failed. In 1851, two missionaries, John Horden and E. A. Watkins, were sent by England. The first mission house was built by Watkins in 1855 and used as a schoolhouse and church. Despite this effort, he was removed a year later after having very little success with the Natives. John Hordon, on the other hand, was much more successful in the south of James Bay. He and James Evans built a schoolhouse in 1854, and in the 1860s a church was built. "The Anglican religion was firmly established in James Bay, and when the diocese of Moosonee was created in 1872, he was made first bishop."[28] The Anglicans were responsible for the education of the children from 1880s to the late 1940s.

Catholics were allowed to organise their first mission in 1863, where there were no Protestants operating. They did not want the presence of the two religions to confuse any Natives. The HBC, although they had originally wanted the missionaries, found that the missions were costing them money. They did not expect that the missionaries would bind the Natives by marriage, and that these unions would create dependents for the HBC. The Catholic religion did not allow polygamous unions; therefore, when they married, they left the "other" women and children dependent on the HBC. "However, by 1879 differences seem to have been resolved and company officials seem to have accepted the benefits of a missionary presence."[29]

A new faith was not all that the missionaries brought along with them to James Bay. Denys Delâge speaks of this as unequal trade, but this time it is not supplies for furs, but the transfer of germs. In this case Natives had nothing to give and all to take. They were not immune to the children's diseases. Many were killed by diseases such as yellow fewer, cholera, chicken pox, and mumps. Delâge explains that these diseases did not exist in North America, because the migration from the Bering Strait was gradual and took place in an arctic climate where germs do not reproduce very easily. The viruses travelled quickly and soon reached those who had not encountered any Europeans, through trading with the middlemen. Half of the Native population was reduced by this phenomena, and some bands were left with only one-tenth of their population, either directly or indirectly. By indirectly it is meant that the population in an area would be weakened by the sickness, and when it had finally left, they had no time to hunt and, therefore, became malnourished and hence more susceptible to other viruses. The diseases also posed a threat to the Native culture by killing the most productive generation and those who held the secrets of the oral traditions. Natives began to accuse the whitemen of witchcraft. Missionaries were the most suspected, because they would hurry to baptise children before the children died. The number of deaths was greater among the Natives converted to Christianity than for those hunters remaining at large. As soon as they would enter a new settlement, one of the childhood diseases would spread. The animals brought from Europe would spread the diseases to other animals through the food chain, and eventually to the Natives.

The following chapter will discuss the influences of the missionaries, in particular how the schooling system manipulated the James Bay Natives. For now, it is important to remember that the missionaries came by request of the HBC, and they were largely responsible for bringing epidemics into the area. To conclude this section, some of the government policies that were implemented between 1600 and 1920 will be briefly examined.

Wallace Clement, Ralph Matthews, and Henry Veltmeyer all agreed that Canada's dependence stemmed from its historical background, when it was dependent on its mother country, and whereby its political and economic structures became British. They claim that as Canada began to detach itself from Britain and began trading more with its neighbour, it became more dependent on the United States. Hence, because of this increased dependence, regional disparities were accentuated. Clement believes this occurred because the "regional economies are tied to national economies and national ones to international ones," thus creating a chain.[30]

Although Canada did not begin to transfer its economic allegiance from Britain to the United States until later, the war of

1812 marked a period of considerable change for Natives. After this war, Canada was no longer threatened by the United States' bringing a large migration of British in search of the promised agricultural land. "From 1814 to 1851, the population of Upper Canada skyrocketed to 952,000 from 95,000."[31] The Natives were no longer a majority and were no longer needed for military or economic purposes. They quickly lost their power, while the Canadian government proceeded to attempt to assimilate them. The next century and a half saw the dawn of many new laws created by the government in the hope of assimilation. For example, in 1857, the "then-Province of Canada offered the vote and 20 hectares of land to those who were educated, debt-free and of good moral character." In exchange, Natives had to give up their status.[32] "In 1869, federal bureaucrats were empowered to depose traditional Indian leaders for 'dishonesty, intemperance or immorality'."[33] That same statute stipulated that Indian women who married non-Indians lost their status.[34] Federal representatives replaced the traditional leaders with elected band councils. Those Natives who had agricultural products to sell needed permits to do so; they also needed permits to leave the reserves in western Canada. Natives were not allowed to wear Native dress off the reserves. "Under the terms of the first Indian Act, which took effect in 1876, Indians lost their status if they became doctors, lawyers, or ministers."[35] From 1894, Natives were forced to send their children to schools run by missionaries (the effect this law had on Natives will be discussed in the next chapter). "Finally, because the Royal Proclamation of 1763 stipulated that Indians could cede title to their lands only to the Crown, Indians could not mortgage their reserve lands to obtain capital for economic projects."[36]

These are a few of the laws that were institutionalised and that made Natives dependent on the centre. The next chapter will examine these more carefully, along with their effects on the James Bay Cree. The slow increase in dependency was examined through each phase covered, from the creation of the HBC to the influence of the Mission and the government. Combining all of these influential factors, one comes to understand the reasons why the Cree of James Bay speak English in a province where the majority of the population is francophone. Their "early involvement with the English Hudson's Bay Company, the Anglican Church, the Federal Government, and English language education, has resulted in a position of social isolation within Roman Catholic, French-speaking Québec society."[37] They are even more distanced from their provincial government than are their counterparts: there is a religion and a language that divides them. Contrary to what many believe, they are bilingual: they speak Cree and English.

In Marxist terms, the periphery represents the cheap labour and the raw materials of the centre. In the past, the centre would take hold of these resources by conquering these territories. Establishing themselves as mother countries, they assured themselves an endless supply of resources and raw materials from the peripheral countries. Whether these products are agricultural or mineral, these regions are stripped for the benefit of others. In the case of the James Bay area, there is no doubt that the land was stripped of its animals to benefit Europeans, but in this case the land was not the only thing that was stripped. The Cree were stripped of their status, of their organisational process, and of their language, among other things. The perfect example of the systematic stripping of the James Bay area, the James Bay Hydroelectric Project, will be discussed later in this book.

The changes the James Bay Cree experienced between the two periods described in this chapter were tremendous. Changes began when the Hudson's Bay Company established trading posts in the area. From then on, the lives of the Cree were never the same. Their hunting patterns were altered by the HBC's policies, such as beaver conservation and the allocation of land and posts to families. They began relying more and more on the posts and hunted less and less. The emergence of the fur trade in eastern Canada also changed the existing relationships that the Natives had with other nations. The Iroquois, who wanted more pelts to trade, waged war with the surrounding nations, many of whom were pushed north into the James Bay area. When the first European traders arrived in the region, they found that most Natives were scared of attacks from the Iroquois. Despite the fact that many will say that these nations fought amongst themselves for more "ridiculous" reasons, the fact remains that they were not fighting to the point of extinction. They would only fight when the conditions were good. If food was lacking in one year, it was not unheard of that they would "suspend" the war. Moreover, once the Europeans arrived with their new economic system, nations would fight others who were weak from epidemics. Therefore, worst of all, they would often fight wars that were not their own. They would sign trade agreements with the English or the French, pledging their military support at the same time.

Many argue that these changes are part of a natural evolution and that Natives of Canada could not continue to live in teepees year round, while sustaining themselves by hunting. Nevertheless, the changes would not have occurred as quickly, even though, sooner or later, they would have come into contact with the outside world. Here again, it does not mean that these nations would have adopted a capitalist system with European values. The real problem with these changes is that they made the James Bay area a periphery, and by doing so made its residents dependent on the centre.

The actions of the HBC, the missionaries, and the government have, in fact, made the Cree dependent on the centre. They were made dependent by having their self-sufficiency removed. As the HBC found themselves with more dependents after each policy they would make, so did the federal government. Peripheral areas and countries are created by the core, not by the members of the periphery, and nor are they part of a natural process of development. As mentioned earlier, there are internal as well as external factors, but the internal factors did not begin to take effect until the core began creating the periphery.

The relationship between the James Bay area and the core is a dependent one. Dos Santos defines a dependent relationship as follows: "some countries (the dominant ones) can expand and can be self-sustaining, while other countries (the dependent ones) can do this only as a reflection of that expansion."[38] An example of this was described in this chapter: when the HBC ascribed parcels of land to each family and a post for each of these hunting families, they took away some of the independence that the hunters possessed. From this point on, the HBC made it very difficult for hunters to seek better deals elsewhere. They could only expand as far as the HBC would let them.

Others may argue that the James Bay area is not one that is underdeveloped, hence a periphery, but merely an undeveloped region of Canada. Rosemary and Ray Bromley outline the distinction of the terms "underdeveloped" and "undeveloped." Development in undeveloped countries would occur when the self-reliance was maintained while developing. Undeveloped countries have access to development perhaps more easily because they have self-reliance, and they are not controlled by outside economic and political powers. These undeveloped countries have not been colonized. By this definition, nothing would be further from the truth to say that the James Bay area is "undeveloped." This region has become a periphery in the true sense of the word: nothing but a source for raw materials ready to be extracted for the sole benefit of the centre.

The next chapter will continue to examine these issues, but it will proceed in a different fashion. It will not discuss events in a chronological fashion, but will discuss the different forms of dependence that have emerged from the events of the 320 years described above. Political and economic dependence will be discussed as well as the many social problems that now plague the

Cree. The long term effects of the actions taken by the HBC, the missionaries, and the government will be examined.

Notes

1. Knight, Roff. *Ecological Factors in Changing Economy and Social Organization among the Rupert House Cree.* Anthropology Papers, National Museum of Canada, Department of the Secretary of State, Ottawa, no.15, March, 1968, p.19.
2. Allahar, Anton L. *Sociology and the Periphery: Theories and Issues.* Garamond Press, Toronto, 1989, p.85.
3. Janigan, Mary. "Lonely Cries of Distrust: Anger and Pain Fuel Native Claims." *Maclean's*, vol. 105, no. 11, March 16, 1992:22-24, pp.22-23.
4. Ibid.
5. Francis, Daniel and Toby Morantz. *Partners in Furs: A History of the Fur Trade in Eastern James Bay 1600-1870.* McGill-Queen's University Press, Kingston and Montréal, 1983, p.13.
6. Wright, J.V. *Quebec Prehistory*, National Museum of Man, Van Nestrand Reinhold Ltd.,Toronto, 1979, p.79.
7. Francis, Daniel and Toby Morantz. *Partners in Furs: A History of the Fur Trade in Eastern James Bay 1600-1870*, p.12.
8. Richardson, Boyce. *Strangers Devour the Land.* Douglas and McIntyre Ltd., Vancouver, 1991, pp.128-129.
9. Ibid., p.34.
10. Tanner, Adrian. *Bringing Home Animals: Religious Ideology and Mode of Production of the Mistassini Cree Hunters*, Social and Economics Studies No. 23, Institute of Social and Economic Research, Memorial University of Newfoundland, C. Hurst and Co. (Publishers) Ltd., London, 1979, p.192.
11. Ibid., p.187.
12. Delâge, Denys. *Le Pays renversé: Amérindiens et Européens en Amérique du Nord-Est: 1600-1664.* Boréal, Compact, Québec, 1991, p.41-45.
13. Francis, Daniel and Toby Morantz. *Partners in Furs: A History of the Fur Trade in Eastern James Bay 1600-1870*, p.23.
14. Roxborough, Ian. *Theories of Underdevelopment.* The Macmillan Press Ltd., London, 1983, p.66.
15. Delâge, Denys. *Le Pays renversé: Amérindiens et Européens en Amérique du Nord-Est: 1600-1664*, p.89.
16. Ibid., p.92.
17. Francis, Daniel and Toby Morantz. *Partners in Furs: A History of the Fur Trade in Eastern James Bay 1600-1870*, p.49.
18. Ibid., p.42.
19. Ibid., p.45.
20. Knight, Roff. *Ecological Factors in Changing Economy and Social Organization among the Rupert House Cree*, p.36.
21. Casanova and Wolpe in Roxborough, Ian. *Theories of Underdevelopment*, p.90.
22. Francis, Daniel and Toby Morantz. *Partners in Furs: A History of the Fur Trade in Eastern James Bay 1600-1870*, p.129.
23. Ibid.
24. Ibid., p.130.

25. Allahar, Anton L. *Sociology and the Periphery: Theories and Issues*, p.90.
26. Francis, Daniel and Toby Morantz. *Partners in Furs: A History of the Fur Trade in Eastern James Bay 1600-1870*, p.27.
27. Ibid., p.32.
28. Ibid., p.163.
29. Ibid., p.164.
30. Clement, in Allahar, Anton L. *Sociology and the Periphery: Theories and Issues*, p.98.
31. Janigan, Mary. "Lonely Cries of Distrust: Anger and Pain Fuel Native Claims," p.23.
32. Ibid.
33. Ibid.
34. Ibid.
35. Ibid.
36. Ibid.
37. Tanner, Adrian. *Bringing Home Animals: Religious Ideology and Mode of Production of the Mistassini Cree Hunters*, p.204.
38. Allahar, Anton L. *Sociology and the Periphery: Theories and Issues*, p.89.

Chapter 3

Effects of Dependency: First Nations in Canada

The previous chapters of this book have already discussed Wallace Clement's belief in the existence of underdeveloped regions within Canada. Clement found that Canada was divided into the industrial core and the hinterland, with industrial Canada being found between Windsor and Montréal. Even though there are other industrial pockets throughout the country, there are some regions that are clearly "underdeveloped": the Atlantic provinces and the northern parts of the country. These regions have wealth, but it is a wealth of natural resources, not financial institutions or production plants. Wages and employment rates remain low in these regions, whose only source of income is from raw materials. Ralph Matthews described the consequences of this underdevelopment, pointing out the neglect of social development, the substandard schools, hospitals, and housing, and the generally lower standard of living than Canadians who live in the "golden triangle" (Toronto-Montréal-Ottawa).[1]

This chapter will discuss the consequences of underdevelopment for First Nations Citizens in Canada using the dependency theory and building on the discussion of how the Cree of James Bay came to be a periphery. It will demonstrate the consequences of underdevelopment for the Cree of James Bay and all First Nations Citizens in Canada.

The consequences of underdevelopment will be grouped into three sections. The first section, entitled "Being Marginal," will examine income, housing conditions, and levels of employment. The second section, entitled "Undeveloped versus Underdeveloped: Definition of Quality of Life," will take a close look at the levels of violence, suicide rates, substance abuse, and health problems. "Internal versus External Factors" is the final section of this chapter, where external influences will be described when examining the dominant laws, politics, and the educational system. This chapter will provide statistics and examples from First Nations Citizens across the country, including the Cree of James Bay. This is done in the hopes that one will realize that the situation experienced by the Cree is not unique to them. The historical description that was provided in the previous chapter, except for some specific details, could very well apply to other First Nations bands. The next chapter of this book will return to the specific example of the James Bay Cree, by referring to the James Bay Hydroelectric Project.

It is important to note that even though no direct comparisons between First Nations bands will be made, there is a general trend across the country. Bands that are closer to industrial areas are less marginalised. They do not experience the economic and social isolation that plague the bands located in the hinterlands. First Nations bands in the south have better employment opportunities, economic development, education, and health facilities than bands in the north.

The Mohawks at Kanasatake, for example, can work and go to school while still residing on the reserve. They obtain better prices for construction and household products, because they are not an isolated community, and there are no additional costs for transportation of the goods they consume. Therefore, when examining provincial statistics, it is important to remember that the First Nations bands in the north have numbers that are less favourable.

In the same light, First Nations women are the most disadvantaged. When studying the statistics comparing registered Indian women and men with all other Canadian women and men, registered Indian women are always the worst off. Their employment levels, income, and education are much lower. No section is dedicated to the situation of the First Nations women; however, reference to their condition will be made whenever appropriate. This is just a reminder that when looking at statistics across Canada one should consider gender, regional differences in terms of provinces, as well as the geographical relationship with the south.

Geoffrey York summarises the changes that the Shamattawa Cree of northeastern Manitoba have undergone since World War II. Their situation is identical to that of the James Bay Cree. York reviews these changes as follows:

> The [Shamattawa Cree] continued their nomadic life of hunting and trapping until the 1940s. Then, as they were gradually drawn into the bureaucratic world of compulsory education and welfare payments, they were required to settle at a fixed location. A federal school was built, and the children were required to attend. To avoid the breakup of their families, and to ensure they received their social assistance cheques, the Shamattawa Cree were forced to settle at the site where they live today. Soon, as fur prices in Europe dropped drastically, their trapping fell into decline and they became dependent on government assistance. Their traditional culture was broken and replaced by a new one.[2]

Most First Nations Citizens in the north were forced to give up their nomadic lifestyle and to settle, in order to receive government transfer payments, upon which they became dependent once their furs had lost most of their exchange value.

First Nations Citizens were made dependent not only through social assistance, but also because "many of the efforts at development of Indian human and natural resources have been consistently biased in favour of Canada's more industrially advanced sector."[3] This idea was given recognition in the 1967

Canadian Government Special Planning Secretariat report, *Profile of Poverty in Canada*, which states: "These people [Indians] were useful to the whites as the labour force of the fur industry, but they were not given the opportunity to compete with whites on their own terms ... for the odds were too heavy. What were these multiple interlocking constraints limiting Indian development, and how have they affected their present economic, social, and political conditions?"[4] This last question is the backbone of each of the following sections. The first section will observe the effects on economic conditions, the second on the social conditions, and the last section on the political system First Nations Citizens are now facing after centuries of domination.

Being Marginal

This section examines the current economic conditions of First Nations Citizens of Canada. Their housing conditions and employment levels will be discussed in order to provide a global picture. These are indicators that have a profound influence over the social conditions of these peoples, and, therefore, should not be overlooked. Geoffrey York states that the social problems that plague First Nations Citizens are part of a bigger problem:

> While better health programs can help alleviate the problems on the reserves, they cannot eliminate them. Sickness and violence on Indian reserves are just symptoms of the larger problems of poverty and underdevelopment. The *Indian Act*, with its restrictions on Native autonomy, and the reserve system, with its patchwork of tiny reserves on infertile land, have locked Indians into a cycle of unemployment, overcrowding, poor health, and dependence on welfare.[5]

As are all residents of underdeveloped regions, the First Nations Citizens of Canada are marginalised. Their income, employment, and housing conditions will be compared to that of "non-Native" Canadians.

According to the United Nations Development Program (UNDP), income is in fact a means and not an end. Income can buy medical supplies or illegal drugs, depending on the society using the money, not the amount of funds available. Residents of a country with modest income can have a good quality of life, while a wealthy country can have deplorable living conditions. The UNDP also adds that the rate of growth is not indicated by income levels alone. One must also consider if the income is invested back into the country.[6] When examining the numbers that represent the income of First Nations Citizens in Canada, one must remember that there is too little for them to reinvest in their community; furthermore, the power to make budgetary decisions is not theirs.

First Nations Citizens living on reserves are the most marginalised. In 1986, they reported earning half of what the general population (non-Native) earned. This is not surprising, since the majority of the Canadian population resides near the industrial centres; however, if geographical location were the only factor involved in determining the average individual income, then registered Indians residing on reserves should have the same income as the general population living near reserves. This is not the case. In the 1986 census, the general population living near reserves reported approximately 30 percent more in average individual income than registered Indians residing on reserves. The registered Indians living off reserves also reported 30 percent less individual income than the general population (Table 1). This indicates that distance from the centre is not the only factor involved, and that education and racism are indicators that should also be considered. These will be examined in the third section of this chapter.

Table 1
Average Individual Income of Registered Indian and General Population

Province	Registered Indian Pop.		Average Individual Income ($)		
	On Res.	Off Res.	Total	General Pop.	Pop. Near Res.
Quebec	9,900.00	13,400.00	10,700.00	17,100.00	13,700.00
Canada	9,300.00	11,000.00	9,900.00	18,200.00	14,700.00

INAC customized data based on 1986 Census of Canada; Populations 15 years and over who received income during 1986; General population: Total population 15 yrs of age and over less registered Indians; Quantitative Analysis and Socio-Demographic Research. *1986 Census Highlights on Registered Indians: Annotated Tables.* (DIAND) Ottawa: Minister of Supply and Services Canada, 1989, p.25.

Table 2
Percentage of Registered Indian Population On And Off-reserve

Province	Place of Residence of Population	
	On Reserve	Off Reserve
Quebec	81.5%	18.5%
Canada	62.4%	37.6%

INAC customised data based on 1986 Census of Canada; Reported place of residence as of June 3, 1986; Quantitative Analysis and Socio-Demographic Research. *1986 Census Highlights on Registered Indians: Annotated Tables.* (DIAND) Ottawa: Minister of Supply and Services Canada, 1989, p.11.

Given that registered Indians residing on reserves have less income, it would be interesting to know just how many live off reserves in Canada. Over 80 percent of registered Indians in Québec lived on reserves in 1986. At the same time, just under 40 percent lived off reserves in Canada (Table 2).

James Frideres states that Natives are dependent on the centre because "their reserves are treated as geographical and social hinterlands for White exploitation. White-controlled businesses exploit nonrenewable primary resources such as oil, minerals, water, and forest products, and ship them to urban industrial centres for processing."[7] Because of this exploitation, First Nations Citizens remain exporters of natural resources, which has always meant dependence and exploitation for every country focusing on primary level exports.

Norman Chance argues that the "economically deprived Indian" has no choice but to rely on "supplementary welfare checks and government rations [which] give him almost no room to manoeuvre."[8] "Without land, money, education, language skills, and other attributes that might assist him in maintaining some control over his environment, he is largely forced by the dictates of his economic condition to accept whatever subsistence income is available, whether it be hunting, trapping, or low paying wage labour."[9] One way of determining the degree of dependence of First Nations Citizens is to examine the origin of their major sources of income. In 1986, 50 percent of registered Indians residing on reserves reported that their major source of income was government transfer payments, while only 20 percent of the general population reported the same. Only 55 percent of registered Indians residing off reserves reported employment income as their major source of income, compared to 70 percent of the general population (Table 3).

As mentioned earlier, it is important to realize that even though these statistics are grim, many First Nations Citizens are even more marginalised. In 1986, registered Indian women earned two-thirds of the income earned by registered Indian men.[10] Geographical location in relation to the centre has a great influence on the wages of First Nations Citizens. In 1981, registered Indians residing on reserves earned an average individual income of $8,700.00,[11] while the Mistassini Cree earned only $2,556.00. Those living off reserves in Québec earned three times more than the Waswanipi Cree in 1981.[12] The general population in Québec, meanwhile, earned $12,500.00, which was three times more than the earnings of the Eastmain Cree.[13] The Rupert House Cree

Table 3

Percentage of Registered Indian and General Populations with Income Whose Major Source of Income is from Employment or Government Transfer Payments

Province	Employment				
	Registered Indian Pop.		Total	General Pop.	Pop. Near Res.
	On Res.	Off Res.			
Quebec	42.0%	56.9%	45.1%	67.1%	56.8%
Canada	48.1%	55.6%	50.9%	71.0%	62.7%

Province	Government Transfer Payments				
	Registered Indian Pop.		Total	General Pop.	Pop. Near Res.
	On Res.	Off Res.			
Quebec	53.9%	37.2%	50.4%	24.2%	36.6%
Canada	48.4%	40.9%	45.6%	19.4%	28.2%

INAC customised data based on 1986 Census of Canada; Major Source of Income: that income component which constitutes the largest proportion of the total income of an individual; Employment: includes wages, salaries and self-employment; Government Transfer Payments: refers to income from all cash transfer payments from all levels of government e.g. family allowances, unemployment insurance, and cash welfare; General population: total population 15 years of age and over less registered Indians; Quantitative Analysis and Socio-Demographic Research. *1986 Census Highlights on Registered Indians: Annotated Tables.* (DIAND) Ottawa: Minister of Supply and Services Canada, 1989, p.27.

reported receiving 44 percent of their total income from government transfer payments; in the same year the national average for registered Indians was 17 percent.[14] In 1981, the non-Native population in Canada reported receiving 8 percent of their income from government transfer payments; that is, almost five times less than the Eastmain Cree[15] (Table 4).

It is also important to realize that the amounts shown above do not have the same buying power as in the south. In isolated communities, the price of goods is much higher. Like the James Bay Cree, the Shamattawa Cree see the cost of transportation increase the price of their goods. For example, in 1990, "a litre of

Table 4
Income ($)

	Great Whale	Eastmain House	Rupert	Waswanipi	Mistassini
Wages and Other Renumeration	935,233	843,664	1,871,150	2,676,594	704,843
Transfer Payments	576516	520,722	1,479,771	372567	141,273
Total Income	1,5117,49	1,364,386	3,350,921	6,401,861	2,119,116
Transfer P. % of Total Income	38.14	38.17	44.16	5.82	6.67
Average Income Per Person	3,827.00	4,147.00	3,542.00	3,195.00	2,556.00
Average Income Per Household	18,214.00	18,690.00	18,720.00	20,006.00	16,054.00

In 1981; Transfer Payments: Family Allowances, Unemployment Insurance, Social Aid, Old Age Security, I.S.P. for Hunters; Beaulieu, Denis. *The Crees and Naskapes of Quebec: Their Socio-Economic Conditions.* Direction des Communications du Governement du Québec, 1984, p.36.

milk [cost] $2.08 — more than double the price in Winnipeg. A loaf of bread [went] for $1.79, and a 284-millilitre can of soup [was] $1.24.[16] Gasoline was $1.80 per litre and a plain windbreaker for a young boy was $73.98.[17] Another reason for these high prices is the monopoly held by the Hudson's Bay stores. They are the dominant chain of stores supplying the isolated communities of the north.

It is important to recognise the financial position of First Nations Citizens, since this position has great impact on social conditions. For example, "there is a proven link between level of income and health status. A look at historical incomes in constant dollars shows that the average incomes of status Indians are decreasing. This fact has serious implications for the general health status and nutrition of status Indians in Canada."[18]

There is a direct link between the low incomes of First Nations Citizens and their high level of unemployment. In 1986, the

Census demonstrated that the general population of Canada was twice as likely to be employed as were the registered Indians living on reserves. In the same year, registered Indians residing off reserves in Canada were one-third more likely to be employed. In Québec, registered Indians living off reserves were four percentage points less likely to be employed than was the rest of the population residing near reserves (Table 5).

The following statistics include the Crees, who are hunters and trappers, making this occupation that of a significant number of the Cree labour force. One should keep this in mind when looking at the statistics, which compare the Cree and other Canadian work force groups. In 1981, only 22 percent of the Waswanipi Cree participated in the labour force, while 52 percent of the general population of Québec participated in the labour force.[19] In the same year, 31 percent of registered Indians in Québec were employed, while only 26 percent of the Rupert House Cree participated in the labour force (Table 6).[20] "Unemployment rates for Indians are presently about 2.5 to 3 times higher than the national rate."[21]

The James Bay Cree are more fortunate than First Nations Citizens residing in urban areas, because they can supplement their employment income by hunting and trapping. The next chapter will discuss this right, which they have over the hunting grounds of the James Bay area. It is also important to remember the types of jobs the 38 percent of employed registered Indians in Canada hold.[22] They have part-time employment, which is seasonal; hence, they have no job security, and "in seasonal jobs, Natives are often discriminated against ... Highly skilled Indian men employed by mining-exploration companies as line-cutters and stakes never receiving the same pay or good working conditions that Whites received."[23]

The level of employment has a direct influence over the quality of life of First Nations Citizens. "The unemployment rate at Shamattawa exceeds 80 percent. Of the band's population of

Table 5
Employment Rates for the Registered Indian and General Population

Province	Employment Rate				
	Registered Indian Pop.				
	On Res.	Off Res.	Total	General Pop.	Pop. Near Res.
Quebec	25.2%	41.1%	28.4%	51.4%	44.0%
Canada	28.2%	36.8%	31.4%	59.8%	51.8%

INAC customized data based on 1986 Census of Canada; Populations 15 years of age and over; General population: Total population 15 years of age and over less registered Indians; Quantitative Analysis and Socio-Demographic Research. *1986 Census Highlights on Registered Indians: Annotated Tables.* (DIAND) Minister of Supply and Services Canada, 1989, p.21.

Table 6
Native Labour Force

	Great Whale	Eastmain	Rupert House	Waswanipi	Mistassini
Governments					
Federal	0 (0.0%)	2 (1.3%)	3 (0.8%)	0 (0.0%)	0 (0.%0)
Prov.	19 (10.7%)	8 (5.3%)	1 (0.3%)	1 (0.3%)	5 (0.6%)
Organizations					
Reg.	40 (22.6%)	27 (17.9%)	39 (9.8%)	34 (9.1%)	72 (9.2%)
Local	17 (9.6%)	8 (5.3%)	6 (1.5%)	1 (0.3%)	16 (2.0%)
Enterprise					
Native	1 (0.6%)	4 (2.6%)	38 (9.5%)	46 (12.3%)	150 (19.1%)
Non-Nat.	8 (4.5%)	7 (4.6%)	15 (3.8%)	0 (0.0%)	16 (2.0%)
Hunters/Trappers	54 (30.5%)	74 (49.0%)	159 (39.9%)	185 (49.3%)	442 (56.4%)
No. of Unemployed	38 (21.5%)	21 (13.9%)	137 (34.4%)	108 (28.8%)	83 (10.6%)
Total	177 (100%)	151 (100%)	398 (100%)	375 (100%)	784 (100%)

In 1982; Beaulieu, Denis. *The Crees and Naskapes of Quebec: Their Socio-Economic Conditions.* Direction des Communications du Governement du Québec, 1984, p.38.

about seven hundred people, more than one-third are essentially homeless — sharing the overcrowded homes of friends or relatives, or living in shacks or decaying houses that desperately need replacement."[24] Their limited income forces them to heat their homes with wood stoves "constructed from old oil drums."[25] These methods of heating, combined with poor housing and overcrowding, increase the risks of fires.

Statistics Canada defines a crowded dwelling as a home that has more than one occupant per room. "By that standard, 36 percent of all households on Indian reserves are overcrowded, according to the Ekos study. By comparison, only 2 percent of the Canadian population lives in overcrowded conditions."[26] In 1986, 37 percent of registered Indians living on reserves in Québec reported occupying crowded dwellings, compared to 4 percent of the non-registered population residing near reserves. Registered Indians not living on reserves in Canada were approximately eighteen times more likely to live in crowded dwellings (Table 7). Some may argue that First Nations Citizens choose to live this way, that it is part of their culture to live with their extended families and friends; however, it is not their culture but their poor income that determines if they will have a heating system in their homes.

In 1986, 38 percent of registered Indian dwellings located on reserves in Canada reported not having a central heating system. A central heating system is defined by Statistics Canada as a steam or hot water furnace, forced air or installed electric heating system. Dwellings occupied by registered Indians off reserves in Canada were almost twice as likely to report having a home without a central heating system, while registered Indians in Québec were more than three times as likely than the general population to report living in a home without a central heating system (Table 8). Geoffrey York reports that "the housing on many reserves is barely above the level of shelter in a Third World village."[27]

Table 7
Percentage of Occupied Private Dwellings Which Have More Than One Person Per Room

Province	% of Dwellings which Have More than One Person Per Room				
	Registered Indian Dwellings			General	Dwel. Near Res.
	On Res.	Off Res.	Total		
Quebec	36.7%	6.9%	26.1%	1.5%	3.9%
Canada	28.9%	11.3%	20.3%	1.7%	2.6%

INAC customized data based on 1986 Census of Canada; For statistical purposes, a dwelling which has more than one person per room is said to be crowded; General Dwelling: Total dwellings less the dwellings of the registered Indians.; Quantitative Analysis and Socio-Demographic Research. *1986 Census Highlights on Registered Indians: Annotated Tables*. (DIAND) Ottawa: Minister of Supply and Services Canada, 1989, p.29.

Table 8
Percentage of Occupied Private Dwellings Without a Central Heating System

Province	% of Dwellings Without a Central Heating System				
	Registered Indian Dwellings			General	Dwel. Near Res.
	On Res.	Off Res.	Total		
Quebec	17.5%	8.6%	14.3%	5.3%	15.9%
Canada	37.5%	9.5%	23.8%	5.3%	13.9%

INAC customized data based on 1986 Census of Canada; Central Heating System: steam or hot water furnace, forced air or installed electric heating system; General Dwellings: Total dwellings less the dwellings of the registered Indians; Quantitative Analysis and Socio-Demographic Research. *1986 Census Highlights on Registered Indians: Annotated Tables*. (DIAND) Ottawa: Minister of Supply and Services Canada, 1989, p.31.

Table 9
Demography

	Great Whale	Eastmain	Rupert House	Waswanipi	Mistassini
Cree Residents	395	329	946	829	2004
Persons/ Household	4.76	4.51	5.28	4.17	6.26

In 1982; Beaulieu, Denis. The Crees and Naskapes of Quebec: Their Socio-Economic Conditions. Direction des Communications du Governement du Québec, 1984, p.36.

Table 10
Municipal Services

	Great Whale	Eastmain	Rupert House	Waswanipi	Mistassini
Drinking Water					
Source	River	Wells	River	Wells	Lake
Purification Plant	yes	yes	yes	yes	yes
Treatment	yes	yes	yes	yes	yes
Water Dist. System	yes	yes	yes	yes	yes
Water Truck	1	none	2	none	none
Laundromat	yes	none	yes	none	none
Waste Management					
Sewer System	none	yes	yes	yes	yes
Septic Tanks	none	none	none	none	none
Compactor Trucks	2	1	none	1	none
Fire Protection					
Fire Hydrants	none	none	20	9	16
Fire Truck	1	none	none	none	none

In 1984; Beaulieu, Denis. *The Crees and Naskapes of Quebec: Their Socio-Economic Conditions.* Direction des Communications du Governement du Québec, 1984, p.41.

The situation of overcrowding is also present in the James Bay Cree communities. For example, there were an average of six Cree per room in Mistassini in 1982. These homes are very overcrowded when one considers that the average size home on reserves has two to three rooms at most (Table 9). "Meanwhile, the federal government has argued that it has no legal obligation to provide housing on reserves. It claims that neither the *Indian Act* nor the nineteenth-century treaties make any mention of an Indian right to housing."[28]

When there is overcrowding or inadequate housing and heating systems, many fires break out, and where there are substandard fire-fighting facilities, these fires often lead to death. Geoffrey York summarises the problem as follows:

> Even without the crude heating system, the small wood-frame houses on Indian reserves are firetraps. When a fire begins, they are often destroyed within a few minutes. Deaths are inevitable because on many reserves there is no basic fire fighting equipment. In Manitoba, for instance, only sixteen of the province's sixty Indian bands have enough equipment and trained staff to fight fires properly.[29]

Of the five communities listed in the table below, only three had fire hydrants, and only Great Whale is equipped with a fire truck. Many non-Native villages in the north have a similar shortage in municipal services, but not as severe. In addition, one must consider that the James Bay Cree were never given many choices. Even those who made the choice to move off the reserve are living in crowded dwellings without a central heating system (Table 10).

The link between income, employment, and housing conditions has been established. It has also been demonstrated that First Nations Citizens on and off reserves are marginalised. They are in an unfavourable position compared to other Canadians in every regard. Some argue that the answer to the problem is economic growth; however, as Frideres argues, there is a great difference between economic growth and economic development. Frideres defines the terms as follows: "economic growth refers to an increase in the productive capacity of an area's economy, while economic development reflects a change in the structure of an area's economy, such as movement from primary extractive or agricultural industries to secondary or processing industries."[30] Many First Nations bands in the prairie provinces have experienced economic growth from oil revenues, but they have not had economic development. Their main source of income is from the sale of raw materials. Once these non-renewable sources have been depleted, nothing will remain and income levels will return once again to what they were. In communities that have only experienced economic growth, social problems that plague First Nations Citizens have remained. The royalties from oil do not provide employment, education, and social services, unless these funds are used for economic development. The next section will discuss the related problems of violence, suicide, substance abuse, and health.

Undeveloped versus Underdeveloped: Definition of Quality of Life

When examining the forces that cause dependence, it is important to understand the differences between undeveloped and underdeveloped nations. When basic infrastructures are in place, when a nation only requires economic growth to reach development status, then this nation is undeveloped not underdeveloped. In undeveloped nations, people are conscious of the means to attain good health care and good housing, and they understand the source of their social problems. In addition, they have the power to obtain these basic necessities with a few extra funds from their secondary and tertiary industries. Underdevelopment is the opposite. Underdeveloped nations also have major social problems that plague them, but they have only limited funds available from the sale of raw resources and no power to create change. Underdeveloped nations have not experienced economic development, only sporadic economic growth. It is important to remember that there is an external force that is limiting the development of these underdeveloped nations, unlike the case of undeveloped nations. The last section of this chapter will examine these external forces and the social problems of violence, suicide, health, and substance abuse.

Statistics Canada reported that, as of 1986, death rates on and off reserves by accidents had decreased but were "still far higher than average: up to age 65, Indian women [were] about 4 times as likely as Canadian women to die from accidents or violence."[31] Violence is a serious problem for First Nations bands, yet Geoffrey York reported that in a floor hockey game among teenagers, which lasted for three hours without a referee, he witnessed no "elbowing or slashing or fighting."[32] And yet these teenagers live on a reserve that has been labelled as "the most dangerous community in the province" by southern Manitoba newspapers.[33] York stated that this game he witnessed was much less violent than matches played in high-schools in the south. "The people of Shamattawa are not violent people. By instinct and by disposition, they are peaceful. And yet there are horrifying crimes of violence on the reserve."[34]

Susan Hare, President of the Ontario Native Women's Association (ONWA), opened the preface to the report *A Proposal for Change to Aboriginal Family Violence* by stating that: "It is not possible to find a First Nations or Metis woman in Ontario whose life has not been affected in some way by family violence."[35] "The reasons behind the high incidence of family violence are intimately connected with the poor social, political and economic" conditions.[36] Often the violence leads to death, and, in domestic violence, it is usually the death of the women. The Ontario Native Women's Association reported that 84 percent of the respondents to their study noticed family violence in their community. Furthermore, 24 percent reported personally knowing of family violence which had led to death.[37] The Ontario Native Women's Association reported the following:

> The types of injuries sustained as a result of family violence in Aboriginal communities were charac-

terised as quite severe: 81 percent reported that the victim suffered bruises; 71 percent mentioned cuts and bleeding; 47 percent broken bones; another 47 percent for wounds; 80 percent said mental and emotional breakdowns were the result; and 7 percent mentioned unwanted pregnancy, disfigurement, and disablement as injuries sustained by violence.[38]

Shelters for First Nations women are not only limited in numbers but in cultural sensitivity. The Ontario Native Women's Association states that these victims of family violence must seek shelter in "non-aboriginal" shelters. Most of these shelters are in urban centres far away from the victim's community and family support. "Moreover, the Aboriginal victim of family violence may even experience racism and further victimisation at the shelter."[39]

The social problems that the First Nations citizens have are all related. Alcohol was said to be involved in domestic fights by 44 percent of the respondents to the Ontario Native Women's Association's survey, while 37 percent claimed that it was often present in incidents of family violence.[40] In total, 78 percent of the respondents said that alcoholism was a main cause of domestic violence. When asked what were the other contributing factors, respondents listed the following: "jealousy (67 percent), unemployment (65 percent), poor communications (57 percent), depression (52 percent), people not knowing how to get along (25 percent), exposure to violence as children (22 percent), problems with other family members (20 percent), and 8 percent mentioned such other causes as low self-esteem, drugs, and nerves."[41] The stresses of overcrowded dwellings, low levels of income, and unemployment add to the levels of violence. Some are reported committing crimes just so that they can be arrested to go to jail, where they are fed three times a day, clothed, and sheltered.

Much of the family violence, alcoholism, and suicides originated from the abuse inflicted on students in residential schools. As Mandy Brown, a social worker on the Lytton reserve, states, like any disease these are problems that are transmitted from generation to generation. Brown was repeatedly trying to treat the community members for these problems, without any success. She finally noticed through the family trees of her victims that there was one connecting factor: St. George's School, an Indian residential school near the reserve. Finally, in December 1987, the former dormitory supervisor, Derek Clarke, "pleaded guilty to eleven counts of buggery and six counts of indecent assault."[42] "In his sentencing judgement, Judge William Blair said Clarke was responsible for at least 140 sexual incidents and perhaps as many as 700 incidents or more."[43] In this instance, an entire community was deeply affected by the sexual abuse incurred at the residential school; however, this is not a scenario that is unique to the Lytton reserve. The same thing has happened in residential schools across the country. Every year a new "skeleton" surfaces. These incidents are not only responsible for much of the family violence, but also for the high rates of suicide in First Nations communities. As mentioned earlier, "Indian women are about 4 times as likely as Canadian women to die from accidents or violence."[44] However, "almost 1/5 of these accidents are in fact suicides."[45] The "suicide rate among Indian women is more than double the national average, and shows no signs of decreasing."[46]

When discussing these social conditions, it is important to remember that there are basic human rights that are not being met, one of them being the right to a long and healthy life. "Indians currently live about 10 years less than non-Indians."[47] The United Nations Development Program (UNDP) claims that a long and healthy life is not the only factor involved in human rights. They also claim fundamental right to knowledge and the right to access to proper resources in order to live a comfortable life. In the

UNDP's definition of human development, it states that the right to "political, economic, or social liberty is as important as creativity, productivity, self-respect, and the guaranty of human rights."[48] It has already been demonstrated that the quality of life of First Nations Citizens is not what it should be due to the high levels of violence in these communities.

Next, the large discrepancies between the health and substance abuse of First Nations Citizens as compared to those of other Canadians will be discussed. This examination will demonstrate that the most basic human rights to a certain quality of life are not met for First Nations Citizens. The final section of this chapter will examine the latter part of the UNDP's definition, which refers to the levels of political, economic and social freedoms, the levels of self-respect, and the right to acquire the necessary knowledge to obtain a comfortable living standard.

The health of First Nations Citizens will be examined in this section of this chapter because, like violence, suicide, and substance abuse, it is greatly influenced by levels of income, housing conditions, and unemployment rates. Geoffrey York summarises the major health problem of First Nations Citizens as follows:

> Canada's Native people are still dying from Third World diseases such as tuberculosis, gastroenteritis, and pneumonia — illnesses that rarely cause death among non-Native Canadians. Tuberculosis, for instance, is widespread in Africa and other parts of the Third World, but it is almost never encountered among non-Native Canadians. Yet tuberculosis is still a deadly reality on Indian reserves, occurring ten times as often among Natives as among non-Natives.[49]

Non-Native Canadians rarely die of or even contract tuberculosis, because it is a disease that is linked to housing conditions.

"The statistics suggest that the comparison to the Third World is still valid. In the African country of Tanzania, the TB rate is 50 to 100 per 100,000 people. On Indian reserves in the Prairies, the rate from 1970 to 1981 was 161 per 100,000."[50] Many other diseases also afflict First Nations Citizens: "a study in 1980 found that the number of deaths caused by cirrhosis of the liver at Shubenacadie was fourteen times the national average."[51] First Nations women are more likely than other Canadian women to form diseases related to the circularity system.[52] The various illnesses that First Nations Citizens are prone to indicate other social problems. As tuberculosis indicates poor housing conditions, the high level of stillbirth for First Nations women, which has not decreased in the last ten years, reflects on the "mother's health, nutrition, lifestyle (smoking/drug use), which may indicate a need for improved nutrition and health promotion programs for mothers."[53]

Once the related problems are discovered, it is easier to practice preventive medicine, that is, to improve housing. In order to develop a successful program, it is important to know the group for which it is needed. For example, the age structure of a group can indicate the various needs of the community. "Three times more of the Canadian population than the Indian population is aged 65 and over (12 percent versus 4 percent). On the other hand, over one and a half times more of the Indian population is under 15 (33 percent versus 21 percent)."[54] Hence, First Nations Citizens are going to suffer more from childhood diseases, while other Canadians will have diseases that manifest themselves in later years: for example, circulatory problems and cancers. First Nations women "are aging into their child-bearing ages while Canadian women are aging into retirement. As a result, Indian women will need health services aimed at mothers and children while Canadian women will need services associated with old age."[55]

One of the problems that arises from the health services and the implementation of new programs is that "the health services are provided largely by white nurses and doctors who usually do not know the local Native language or the traditions of Native healing. Their communication with their patients is hampered by the cultural gap."[56] Geoffrey York points out that health programs will never "alleviate the problems on reserves," because "sickness and violence ... are just symptoms of the larger problems of poverty and underdevelopment."[57]

In the next section and chapters, the links between the problems of violence, suicide, health, and substance abuse will be linked to "the *Indian Act*, with its restrictions on Native autonomy, and the reserve system, with its patchwork of tiny reserves on infertile land, [which] have locked Indians into a cycle of unemployment, overcrowding, poor health, and dependence on welfare."[58]

The James Bay Cree suffer from the same illnesses described above. The health care system of the Cree consists of limited nursing stations, which have "few preventative medicine programs or community health programs."[59] There are no doctors stationed in any of the five communities surveyed. Those in need of critical care must be transported to the nearest hospital or "wait for long periods of time for a doctor to come."[60] Prior to the James Bay agreement, health services were "organised and administered by the Department of National Health and Welfare of the Federal Government and were based on a series of nursing stations" (Table 11).[61] The question of health services was an important part of the discussion in the James Bay agreement. The outcome of these talks will be examined in the next chapter, along with mercury poisoning, an illness brought on the Cree by the flooding of the rivers in the James Bay area. During the late 1960s and early 1970s, the government of the province of Québec "was asserting its jurisdiction over the vast territory which had been transferred to it by the Federal Government in 1912."[62] The province funded the construction of the Hospital of Fort George, where there would be practising doctors. This hospital, built in the early 1970s,

Table 11
Health Services

	Great Whale	Eastmain	Rupert House	Waswanipi	Mistassini
Local Facilities					
Hospital Centre	none	none	none	none	none
Nursing Station	yes	yes	yes	yes	yes
No. of Beds	2	2	2	2	2
Personnel					
Physicians	none	none	none	none	none
Nurses	2	2	4	2	4
Interpreters	1	1	2	none	1
Other	none	none	none	none	none
Residents per					
No. of Beds/100	0.51	0.61	0.21	0.24	0.10
Nurses/100	0.51	0.61	0.42	0.24	0.20

In 1984; Beaulieu, Denis. *The Crees and Naskapes of Quebec: Their Socio-Economic Conditions.* Direction des Communications du Governement du Québec, 1984, p.40.

"was administered by an independent corporation whose members included representatives of the Fort George Band."[63]

Substance abuse, especially alcoholism, is a problem often associated with First Nations Citizens. There are high levels of alcoholism in these communities. "Many Native leaders regard alcohol as their number one problem. Recent studies have estimated that alcohol is abused by about 45 percent of New Brunswick Indians, about 38 percent of Saskatchewan Indians, and 50 to 60 percent of northern Manitoba Natives."[64]

The problem with alcohol did not become obvious until after World War II, when the federal government began establishing military bases in remote areas of the country, most often near reserves. Until this time, First Nations Citizens had remained isolated, though their contact with "whites" was increasing dramatically. The federal government introduced social programs, such as housing projects and welfare programs, during this time. This increased the flow of money into Native hands, allowing them to purchase goods outside the reserve for the first time. "When new legislation in the 1950s and 1960s allowed Indians to purchase liquor, much of the newly available cash was spent on alcohol."[65]

At the same time, the exploitation of resources in the hinterland increased dramatically, taking much independence away from First Nations. Residential schools were beginning to have their effect on the communities and the culture. A loss of identity and the sense of being caught between two cultures was transmitted. "The government's new social programs helped create a state of dependence in the Native communities. The Indian population was growing rapidly — too rapidly for most reserves, which were small and had a fixed size. The traditional self-sufficient economy of hunting and trapping fell into decline as a result" of the expanding industries and white settlements.[66] "Indians lost their pride when they could not support their families without a welfare cheque."[67]

The list of causes that pushed First Nations towards alcoholism is long and continues to grow, since many Indians, after World War II, may have started drinking for the reasons listed above. Some are drinking today because drinking has been passed on from one generation to the next. Geoffrey York quotes the statement of Bea Shawanda of the National Native Association of Treatment Directors: "What we are talking about is the grief over a significant loss — the loss of our languages, our culture ... We are acting out that grief through the violence and the alcoholism."[68]

Binge drinking is very common among First Nations Citizens. "A survey of Saskatchewan Indians in 1984 showed that 72 percent consumed five or more drinks each time they drank. Among the Indians of northern Manitoba, the average episode of non-stop drinking lasts for three to seven days."[69] Drinking is also related to the accidental death rates of First Nations Citizens. Geoffrey York summarises the extent of this link:

> Each year, more than 20,000 potential years of life are lost as a result of the effects of alcohol among Canadian Indians. About three-quarters of all deaths caused by accidents, violence, or poisoning among aboriginal people are linked to alcohol. The vast majority of Indian suicides, homicides, fire fatalities, and other unnatural deaths occur while alcohol is being consumed.[70]

Many childbirth defects are caused by the consumption of alcohol by pregnant women. "A medical researcher in British Columbia found that 25 percent of all children at one Indian reserve had birth defects as a result of 'fetal alcohol syndrome,' a condition in which the infants suffer mental retardation or facial abnormalities as a result of heavy alcohol consumption by the mother."[71] The far reaching effects of alcohol abuse are as enormous as the causes of alcoholism in First Nations communities.

Another problem the First Nations bands face is gasoline sniffing. There are many problems that accompany this substance abuse, the most severe of which is finding ways to control the sniffing. Many reserves set up road blocks and search incoming airplanes in order to confiscate all forms of alcohol. Unfortunately, gasoline is a necessity, for boats, trucks, and skidoos. "Children and teenagers sniff [gasoline] to gain a quick escape, a cheap and immediate high — a few minutes of euphoria in a land of poverty and misery."[72] Medical experts claim "that gasoline sniffing is one of the most dangerous addictions in the world."[73] They have concluded that "a single inhalation can be enough to hook a child."[74] The effects are the same as LSD, "procuring euphoria and a state of altered consciousness. Gasoline sniffers often become convinced that they are invincible."[75] Geoffrey York summarises the effects of gasoline sniffing on the youths:

> Once inhaled, gasoline harms the kidneys and liver, and inflicts permanent damage on the nervous system and the brain, especially those parts of the brain that control visual coordination, motor skills, and memory. It impairs the cognitive abilities that would normally permit children to learn. In the early stages of its use as an inhalant, gasoline reduces inhibitions and thus can help to trigger violence. Chronic sniffers become dull and clumsy, shake uncontrollably, and sometimes have difficulty walking. They often become anaemic and suffer weakness in their arms and legs. The emotional and psychological consequences of gasoline sniffing are just as severe: it produces feelings of paranoia, isolation, and indifference toward oneself and others.[76]

Gasoline sniffing is a serious problem that was first noticed in the early 1970s, but the problem has increased. Around 1975, "a survey of Cree and Inuit youths at Great Whale River in northern Québec revealed that 62 percent had sniffed gasoline at least once in the previous six months."[77] In 1986, it was discovered that 70 percent of the children belonging to twenty-five northern Manitoba bands had sniffed gasoline.[78] "About 1,400 of these children were in 'serious trouble' and needed treatment for their addiction."[79] Researchers "found at least four reserves" in northern Manitoba "where parents were sniffing with their children."[80] Some were said to use gasoline to calm their infants. As mentioned earlier, one of the effects of gasoline sniffing is extreme violence. The police and court officials claim that 60-70 percent of juvenile crimes involve gasoline sniffing.[81]

The problem is so serious that there is a name that has been given the death it can cause: "sudden sniffing death syndrome." Death occurs when "the heartbeat of a sniffer becomes irregular because of the chemicals in the inhalants. Then, when he tries to run or fight, adrenalin rushes through his body and his heartbeat becomes even more irregular and uncontrollable. His heart fails and he dies."[82] Many precautions have been taken to try to stop this addiction. The Hudson Bay store stopped selling glue, wood filler, nail-polish remover, felt-tip markers, typewriter correction fluid, and aerosol sprays. It has also stopped selling "potatoes, raisins, yeast, and anything else that can be fermented into alcohol."[83] But as mentioned earlier, it can not stop selling gasoline. Some bands have imposed curfews and "gas patrols." They take down the names of children who are caught and provide a copy to the nursing station and the band council. "In reality, the gas patrol is virtually helpless, since gasoline sniffing is not illegal. The police cannot arrest the sniffers. And the doctors know, from experience, that compulsory medical treatment cannot cure the plague."[84]

Some children start sniffing as early as four years old when they see their brothers and sisters sniffing gasoline. "George Redhead is the supervisor of the gas patrol and the coordinator of the Leonard Miles Memorial Centre. For years, he has been doing his best to fight the surge in gas sniffing. He tries to introduce recreational programs and social activities to keep the children out of trouble. The number of sniffers fluctuates, but the problem never disappears."[85] It is a common belief that if you keep children busy enough with activities they will not find the time into get themselves in trouble. Perhaps one of the reasons why children get into trouble is the lack of facilities to keep busy. Of the five communities surveyed in the James Bay area, not one had a community centre, a library, or an arena; only one had a playground, two had a gymnasium, and three had a skating rink and a ball field (Table 12).

Table 12
Recreation and Leisure

	Great Whale	Eastmain	Rupert House	Waswanipi	Mistassini
Gymnasium	yes	yes	none	none	none
Community Centre	none	none	none	none	none
Library	none	none	none	none	none
Arena	none	none	none	none	none
Skating Rink	none	none	yes	yes	yes
Playground	none	none	none	yes	none
Ball Field	none	none	yes	yes	yes

Source: Beaulieu, Denis. *The Crees and Naskapes of Quebec: Their Socio-Economic Conditions*. Direction des Communications du Governement du Québec, 1984, p.42.

Gasoline sniffing is a serious problem for First Nations Citizens, and according to Dr. Juis Fornazzari, "a neurologist at the Addiction Research Foundation in Toronto and an expert on inhalant abuse," it is a problem that only afflicts the members of minority groups.[86] Many minorities have been found to be inhalant abusers: the First Nations Citizens of Australia and the United States, Hispanics, children of migrant workers, and illegal aliens. "And in almost every case, there is one unifying factor: the young addicts are poverty-stricken members of a community that has been overwhelmed by a more powerful outside culture. They are victims of cultural invasion or dislocation."[87] The dominant culture has destroyed the traditional economy and social organisation. "In each case, members of the minority group are stripped of their identity and their traditional way of life, and they descend into a pattern of self-destructive behaviour. Inhalants are simply the cheapest and most accessible of the weapons of self-destruction."[88] As discussed earlier, the solution is not in stopping the sale of inhalants or in sending all of the children to detoxication centres, but it lies in creating employment and economic opportunities — in other words, to have economic development, not just economic growth. Dr. Tenenbein, a physician, believes that the root of the problem lies in "the social upset, discord, and disharmony. Dependency on welfare [has] given the people of Shamattawa a total lack of self-worth," he says. What could be more depressing than to wait for the government cheque?[89]

Basic human rights are not met for most First Nations Citizens. Quality of life and good health are absent. Some will argue that alcoholism and violence are present in "white" communities as well, but the fact remains that in all instances it has been shown that First Nations people are plagued much more severely than the rest of the Canadian population. They are underdeveloped because their basic human rights are not met, and because they lack many of the basic institutions to render their society healthy. In all cases, one of the common factors behind the sicknesses is the lack of economic development. Some groups receive royalties from the exploitation of their natural resources, while many have only their welfare cheques. This basic existence is not enough to create economic development, nor human development, which requires political, social, and economic freedom, along with the right to creative production and self-respect.

The next section will examine some of the obstacles to economic and human development, two of the fundamental elements for creating a healthy society free of violence, suicide, sickness, and substance abuse.

Internal versus External Factors

As mentioned in the first chapter of this book, the theory of dependency has some extreme versions, which include focusing on either internal or external factors that influence the living conditions of underdeveloped peoples. Some believe that the fault lies either entirely with the external or the internal structures. The tendency chosen for this book claims that it is the fault of both forces. Economic and human development is determined by the actions of both the internal and external actors.

However, this book will not examine the internal factors, but acknowledges their influence. I have done this because of my lack of understanding of the culture and the direction in which most First Nations wish to head and because of the lack of responsiveness by many First Nations Citizens to "non-Native" suggestions; again there is no blame, simply a lack of understanding.

The Ontario Native Women's Association summarises the thoughts of many First Nations People regarding individuals who have tried to alleviate the health problems of their people as follows: "while these studies [written by white people] are well-intentioned, the difficulty is that only an Aboriginal woman can knowledgeably speak on our needs, our cultural perspective, and our hopes for change."[90] Some representatives give this message to "non-Natives" in a much harsher tone. Therefore, in the hopes of not sounding as though I am avoiding the topic of internal causes, I will leave these for others more capable of analysing these factors. The final section of this chapter will concentrate on the external factors that are causing the lack of economic and human development in First Nations communities.

This section will be divided into three parts: the first part will discuss the laws that hamper the development of First Nations Citizens; the second part will examine the political institutions that stand in the way of a healthy society; and the third part will examine the effects of a poor education system that is designed to assimilate those within it.

It has often been argued that there are in fact two justice systems in this country, one for the dominant group and the other for First Nations Citizens. The most famous example is that of Donald Marshall, the son of the Grand Chief of the Micmac Nation in Nova Scotia who was sent to prison for eleven years for a murder he did not commit. But there are many more examples of this, which relate not only to individuals but to the creation of laws.

Some of the individual cases may be found in the incredible statistics on incarcerated First Nations Citizens. "Aboriginal people constitute 10 [percent] of the overall prison population in Canada, and in some provinces more than 32 [percent] of the prison population, while we make up only 2 [percent] of the overall population of the country."[91] The Ontario Native Women's association claim that First Nations Citizens do not respect the police, who are most often "non-Native," and the laws that have been imposed upon them. The members of their community who command the most respect are not police officers but the "Elders and Spiritual leaders — our Grandmothers, our hereditary chiefs, our clanmothers."[92] Statistics demonstrate that there is a change in the police force, and that members of the judicial system have recognised the importance of having Native police officers on reserves. Out of the five communities in the James Bay area, only Great Whale had non-Native officers, and only Great Whale had more non-Native officers than Native. In Great Whale, Native officers were out-numbered three to one (Table 13).

There are reasons why the First Nations' incarceration rate is so high, but, first, there are more examples of the composition of the inmate population across the country. "In Newfoundland and New Brunswick, the Native incarceration rate is four to six times worse than the provincial average. In British Columbia and Alberta, Natives represent 20 to 30 percent of the prison population, even though they represent just 5 percent of the total population."[93] These numbers are bad and are getting worse: "within a few years, Natives will represent 80 percent of the prison population in Saskatchewan."[94] In fact "there is a provincial correctional centre, where 75 percent of the inmates are Native. And there is a women's jail, where 85 percent of the inmates are Native."[95] Some of the reasons for the high level of imprisonment of First Nations

Table 13
Justice

	Great Whale	Eastmain	Rupert House	Waswanipi	Mistassini
No. of Policemen					
Natives	1	1	2	2	4
Non-Natives	3	0	0	0	0
Police Station with two cells	yes	yes	yes	yes	yes
Judicial District of Abitibi	yes	yes	yes	yes	yes

Source: Beaulieu, Denis. *The Crees and Naskapes of Quebec: Their Socio-Economic Conditions.* Direction des Communications du Governement du Québec, 1984, p.42.

Citizens have already been discussed. Some commit crimes in order to get arrested, so that they can improve their living conditions. Many others are incarcerated for violent crimes that they committed while under the influence of alcohol or other narcotics. Others are simply arrested for failing to show up in court, because they can not afford to pay their transportation, which often means a plane trip from the most isolated communities. Others go to jail because they can not pay the fines determined by the courts. "At one provincial jail in Manitoba, up to 60 percent of the Native inmates in 1987 were serving jail terms because they were unable to pay fines."[96] Many have also been incarcerated due to problems that are imbedded in the society, the same problems which led to violence, suicide, and substance abuse. These are problems that can only be solved with human and economic development, with the cooperation of both internal and external institutions.

The laws concerning First Nations Citizens have also helped convince many that there are two justice systems in Canada. The

Royal Proclamation, written in 1763, "stipulated that Indians could cede title to their lands only to the Crown. Indians could not mortgage their reserve lands to obtain capital for economic projects."⁹⁷ Many First Nations Citizens are outraged by the fact that the land they once occupied alone is now not theirs to do with what they please. Not only can they not choose where they will live, having had whites assign them to land, or mortgage the land under Section 29 of the *Indian Act*, but they can be moved at any time, again and again. "Under Section 35 of the *Indian Act*, the federal government has the authority to transfer land on an Indian reserve to a province or municipal government or to a corporation, without obtaining the consent of the Indians who live there."⁹⁸ There are numerous examples of First Nations bands who have been transferred several times in order to push the development of the dominant group. Each displacement brought on worse living conditions, more loss of culture, and an increase in social problems.

There are many more laws that, when enforced, act as external forces slowing down the human and economic development of First Nations Citizens. The right to vote in federal elections, one of the most basic rights, was not granted to First Nations Citizens until 1960. "New Brunswick and Prince Edward Island did not give Indians the franchise until 1963, and Alberta and Québec refused to let Indians vote until 1965 and 1969, respectively."⁹⁹

As with Sections 35 and 29, many other sections of the *Indian Act* restrained the development of First Nations Citizens. "Section 73 allows the federal government to pass regulations to limit hunting and fishing on the reserves, and Section 88 allows provincial governments to put reserves under the jurisdiction of provincial game conservation laws."¹⁰⁰ These sections were merely continuing the tradition of the beaver conservations established in the 1800s. The *Income Tax Act* and the *Indian Act* hindered the economic development of First Nations Citizens. Fields and Stanbury describe one of the effects:

> If Indians choose to undertake economic development of their reserves utilizing the form of a limited company, then they lose the benefit of exemption from taxation as individuals or as a band. Income earned by a corporation wholly owned by Indians is subject to taxation the same as any corporation — even if the income is derived solely from activities on a reserve.[101]

The *Income Tax Act* and the *Indian Act* seem to offer no leeway to the entrepreneurial spirit on reserves. Frideres summarises the laws affecting First Nations Citizens as follows: "The combined effect of the paternalistic restrictions in the *Indian Act* has crippled the economies of most reserves. In 1981, a federal memorandum admitted that the government's policies had created dependent and alienated Indian societies which demonstrate many of the characteristics of underdeveloped nations of Africa, Asia, and Latin America."[102]

Another reason why many believe there are two justice systems in Canada is the fact that judges from the dominant group can overturn the *Bill of Human Rights*. One of the first cases to argue against the legislation using the *Bill of Human Rights* was "The Drybones Case." The lawyers in this case argued that Section 94(b) of the *Indian Act* violated the human rights of First Nations Citizens as stipulated by the *Bill of Human Rights*. This Section, "expressed in plain and unequivocal words [that] an Indian who is intoxicated off a reserve is guilty of an offence."[103] The lawyers argued that Section 94(b) of the *Indian Act* "clearly discriminated against a minority by making its members subject to an offence that applied to no other group."[104] It had been determined in a previous case that the *Bill of Human Rights* could be used only when the legislation needed to be interpreted, and that Section 94(b) needed no interpretation: "the majority ruled that the *Bill of Human Rights* does grant to courts the power to invalidate federal legislation, even when it existed before the bill and was clearly drafted that it required no judicial interpretation."[105] Section 94(b) would later be revised. Many believed that this case would give power to the *Bill of Human Rights* over all legislatures, thereby protecting the human rights of Canadians.

However, this euphoria was short lived. Shortly thereafter "the federal responsibility and power to govern aboriginal people again raised a serious human rights issue...forcing the SCC [Superior Court of Canada] into retreat."[106] The case dealt with Section 12(1)(b) of the *Indian Act*, which stated that any Indian woman who married a non-Indian would automatically lose her Indian status and so would her children. Lavell and Bedard argued that this Section violated the human rights of Ms. Lovelace who was discriminated against on the basis of sex. The Supreme Court of Canada argued that Section 12(1)(b) did not create inequality for women and went back to the previous ruling that "argued that the clarity of the legislation prohibited its being interpreted in any other way, and that the *Bill of Rights* could apply only when legislative provisions were sufficiently vague to require judicial interpretation."[107] Some argued that the previous case did not involve "the internal regulation of lands reserved for Indians" as this case did.[108] "It is, therefore, not difficult to view the judgement as a Court bias favouring administrative convenience for government authorities over the basic rights of individuals.[109]

The Canadian court ruled that Ms. Sandra Lovelace could not return to her reserve after having terminated her marriage to a non-Indian. Left with no other alternative, she brought her case to the International Human Rights Committee. Ms. Lovelace's lawyers argued on the basis of Section 27, which "guarantees minorities the right, in community with other members of their group, to enjoy their own culture, to profess and practice their own religion, or to use their own language."[110] The International Committee found that Canada was violating the human rights of Ms. Lovelace. Her lawyers were certain that Canada would change its legislation rapidly following the ruling from this international court, but this was not the case. Ms. Lovelace "initiated her complaint in 1977, the Committee issued its report in 1981."[111] She finally married an Indian man, thereby reinstating her Indian status and allowing her to return to the reserve. It was not until 1986 that the *Indian Act* was amended with Bill C-31, returning the birthright of women like Ms. Lovelace and their children.

Between 1957 and 1977, Section 12(1)(b) removed the Indian status of 13,000 women and their children, now parents themselves.[112] Frideres explains who was included in Bill-C31:

> This included women who were deleted from the register upon marriage to a non-Indian (Sections 12(1)(b) and 14); individuals deleted at the age of majority because their mothers and paternal grandmothers were not Canadian Indian by birth (Sections 12(i)(a)(iv)); individuals deleted due to husbands'/fathers' enfranchisement (Sections 10 and 109); and any illegitimate children of Indian women who were deleted from the register upon proof of non-Indian paternity (subsection 12(2)).[113]

"Only the first generation of those listed above are eligible for registration."[114] These people have until the year 2003 to reach maturity and apply. If these applicants have children at the time of reinstatement, they can not pass on their status; however, once registered, they can transmit their status to their children born after they were reinstated.

The *Indian Act* and other laws acted as external causes which inhibited the human and economic development of First Nations Citizens. The lack of control over their land has meant displacement and hardship for these people. The *Indian Act*, which removed the Indian status for so many, has meant an extensive loss of culture because they could not live in their communities. In 1986, "90 percent of all Bill C-31 registrants lived off-reserve."[115]

When examining the internal political structures, one can understand how dominant countries still have a hold over peripheral countries or regions. Currently, when most countries have become "independent" of their mother countries, the centre still controls the peripheral regions. They do this by controlling the political leaders. They hold what Edward Herman and Noam Chomsky call "demonstration elections." The centre creates "client states with puppet governments whose financial and military strings are pulled in Washington or London."[116]

"Whites," acting as the centre in the case of Canada, have hampered the development of First Nations Citizens by controlling their political structures. In the late 1800s the Canadian government began "arbitrarily replacing traditional leaders with elected band councils."[117] The centre removed the existing political structures, which were already quite sophisticated. "For example, the Six Nations Confederacy of the Iroquois had a well-established system of chief selection as well as a set of procedures that were used to replace representatives from various nations in the confederacy."[118] The centre attempted "to fix something which was not broken," but the fact is that to "whites" the system did look dysfunctional. It was so much easier to standardise all the peripheral governments to one model, diminishing the task of dealing with different nations each with their own cultures. James Frideres describes the relationship of the *Indian Act* to the new political structures:

> The government system now operating for most bands is that which is prescribed under the terms of the *Indian Act*. The *Indian Act* imposed a band council system of local government. Under these terms,

Indians form a council of chief and council members, who are usually elected by the membership to carry out various administrative duties. The actual duties and responsibilities of the council are also specified in the *Indian Act*.[119]

The "whites" were seeking assimilation and civilization. They forced municipal-like political structures onto First Nations bands, creating a loss of culture and power. Their power is limited by Section 82 "which gives the Indian Affairs minister the authority to disallow bylaws passed by the council."[120] For example, the federal government intervened, in 1979, when the Membertou band in Sydney "passed a bylaw to enforce speed limits on the reserve," because the bylaw exceeded "the scope of the powers enumerated in Section 81 of the *Indian Act*."[121]

The centre solicited the help of Indian agents to enforce the *Indian Act*. Indian agents had the power to "prosecute Indians on the reserves and to preside over band council meetings until the late 1960s."[122] They issued passes needed by First Nations Citizens to leave their allocated reserves and to sell their crops. They prohibited "spiritual ceremonies such as the potlatch and Sun Dance."[123] The power of Indian agents was transferred to federal bureaucrats in the late 1960s. They are the ones controlling the money that reaches the reserves from the Department of Indian and Northern Affairs, "thereby controlling the quality of life of the people who live" in the periphery.[124] This money is spent on government transfer payments, rather than on economic development, and since band councils have no say in the form of funding they receive, First Nations remain dependent on the centre.

Not only does the political structure directly influence economic development, but political and leadership organisation are also influenced by the lack of economic development. Boldt explains this intricate relationship as follows:

> Most striking is the statistic relative to leaders who derive their influence from the economic sector. Not a single Indian leader could be classified as exercising his influence in the economic sector. This provides evidence of the degree to which Indians generally have been excluded from the Canadian economic sector and hence the power structure.[125]

This lack of control over policy and economy are some of the external factors that contribute to the social problems which the First Nations face. The Ontario Native Women's Association claims that "the violent reaction in the family is a reaction against an entire system of domination, lack of respect, and bureaucratic control."[126]

Norman Chance states that the "political constraints impinging on the Cree Indians [of James Bay] are ... damaging to their overall development."[127] The more isolated the reserves, the longer the traditional political structures remained. As early as the 1970s, however, the traditional political leaders were becoming inadequate due to the increase in the "Indian-white relations." These were replaced "by those whose major sources of power reside in their ability to communicate with whites, and, not infrequently, their willingness to implement white directives."[128] The fact remains, however, that even the new leaders do not get to participate in the policy making process; they most often simply reinforce the policies that have already been set by the central governments.

The dominant group changed the political structures of the minorities in order to render them less effective and powerless. This external force has contributed to the position First Nations Citizens find themselves in today. However, the laws and the political structures are not the only external forces; the educational system has been greatly responsible for the social problems of the First Nations.

First Nations Citizens have a much lower level of education than "non-Indians." Statistics Canada defines people who are functionally illiterate as those having less than grade nine education. According to this definition, over 50 percent of the registered Indian population on reserves in Québec was functionally illiterate in 1986, while less than 24 percent of non-Indians had less than grade nine education. Even for registered Indians residing off reserves, the tendencies were similar. In 1986, a little less than a quarter of this population was deemed functionally illiterate, while only 17 percent of the non-Indian population in Canada had less than a grade nine education. While over half of registered Indians living off reserves were functionally illiterate, only 35 percent of the non-Indians living near reserves could be grouped into the same category. Some may point out that the rates are high for registered Indians simply because their population is so young and many have not reached grade nine; however, these percentages are only composed of people who are fifteen years of age or older (Table 14).

First Nations Citizens also have low percentages with respect to high school education. In 1986, less than 20 percent of registered Indians residing on reserves were reported to have at least a high school education, while over 56 percent of the non-Indians of Québec claimed the same. The population residing near reserves, both in Canada and Québec, were twice as likely to have obtained their high school diploma than were registered Indians living on reserves in 1986. As usual, even registered Indians living off reserves were less likely to have high school graduates in their community than did non-Indians in Québec and in Canada: 45 percent compared to 56 percent in Québec, and 38 percent and 56 percent in Canada (Table 15).

Many circumstances help to explain this low education rate and high rates of high school drop-outs. One circumstance is that

Table 14
Percentage of Registered Indian Population and General Populations With Less Than Grade 9 Education

Province	Percentage of Pop. with Less than Grade 9 Education				
	Registered Indian Pop.				
	On Res.	Off Res.	Total	General Pop.	Pop. Near Res.
Quebec	50.7%	28.4%	46.2%	23.8%	34.5%
Canada	44.7%	24.4%	37.2%	17.1%	25.8%

INAC customized date based on 1986 Census of Canada; Populations 15 years of age and over; For statistical purposes, less than grade 9 education is used as a proxy of functional illiteracy; General population: Total population 15 years of age and over less the registered Indians; Quantitative Analysis and Socio-Demographic Research. *1986 Census Highlights on Registered Indians: Annotated Tables.* (DIAND) Ottawa: Minister of Supply and Services Canada, 1989, p.17.

Table 15
Percentage of Registered Indian Population and General Populations With Minimum High School Education

Province	Percentage of Pop. with at Least High School Education				
	Registered Indian Pop.				
	On Res.	Off Res.	Total	General Pop.	Pop. Near Res.
Quebec	19.7%	45.3%	24.9%	56.4%	39.7%
Canada	21.7%	37.5%	27.6%	55.8%	41.9%

INAC customized data based on 1986 Census of Canada; Populations 15 years of age and over; General population: Total population 15 years of age and over less registered Indians; Quantitative Analysis and Socio-Demographic Research. *1986 Census Highlights on Registered Indians: Annotated Tables.* (DIAND) Ottawa: Minister of Supply and Services Canada, 1989, p.19.

First Nations Citizens are a minority, and, like all minority groups, their level of education is much lower. Many argue that this is caused by biased institutions that have low expectancy rates for these children. They are expected to graduate from high school if they apply themselves, while children belonging to the dominant group are expected to continue toward a post-secondary education. However, there are circumstances that are particular to First Nations children, the first being Indians status, and the second being the residential schools. Those wishing a post-secondary education were strongly advised to give up their Indian status. This occurred at the same time that a Bill amending the *Indian Act* was passed stating that Indian children had to go to school, that it was no longer a voluntary act. "Duncan Campbell Scott, Deputy Superintendent General of Indian Affairs, summarised the intent of the amendments:

> Our object is to continue until there is not a single Indian in Canada that has not been absorbed into the body politic, and there is no Indian question, and no Indian department, and that is the whole object of this Bill.[129]

"Indian residential schools, founded and operated by Protestant and Catholic missionaries, were the dominant institution in Indian communities across Canada from the late nineteenth century until the 1960s."[130] First Nations Citizens in western Canada were forced to send their children to "schools run by missionaries," as early as 1894. Until 1945 First Nations children were taken from their communities and educated in residential schools far away from their families. It was not until this date that children were allowed to "travel off the reserve to receive an education."[131] At this time, the legislation forcing children to attend schools was much stronger for First Nations students than for children of the dominant group.

Many people argue that this was, in fact, cultural genocide. These children were taken away from their communities and families, often by force, and placed in isolated residential schools. These schools were more often than not administrated by a practising religious group. This meant that the students were forced to practise a religion that was not their own. They were forbidden to speak "Indian" or to practise any small ceremonial gestures. The horror stories of child abuse and sexual assault in these residential schools are still rearing their ugly heads. These children were caught between two cultures: "whites" tried to assimilate them into a society that was not ready to receive them, while taking away all the skills necessary to function in their own society. The students never had the informal education they required to learn the Indian language, religion, hunting, and gathering. There are two entire generations that have been lost. But this affects more than two generations; it has also affected their children and grandchildren. The children of these lost generations were victims of abuse because of the residential schools. Their parents became abusers and abused them. Their parents had lost much of their culture; therefore, the little informal education they could receive did not come from their broken homes but from their grandparents. Residential schools began vanishing in the 1960s. The loss of culture that occurred in those decades is enormous. At least four generations of First Nations Citizens went through this educational system. The effects of residential schools was so severe that the term "residential-school syndrome" was coined by psychologists. "They compare it to the grief cycle that a person undergoes after the loss of a close relative. But instead of losing a parent or a spouse, the Indians have lost a culture. Something they were born with, a part of their soul, was wiped out by the missionaries and the teachers."[132]

Minority groups are often deprived of their basic human rights. One of these basic rights is education. When the educational system is poor it becomes harmful to the minority group.

Education is a very powerful tool that can be used by the dominant group to control the minority. When the program is not administered fairly it widens the gap between the minority and the dominant groups. Douglas Ray and Vincent D'Oyley stress these points:

> Education was seen as a right, with many references to the Universal Declaration of Human Rights. Paradoxically, it was also recognised that many systems of education have further advantaged the comparatively well educated but neglected the needs of those less educated; thereby deepening the social, economic, and political rifts of society.[133]

The point is that it is not enough for the Canadian government to say it is funding some schools and, therefore, fulfilling its obligations. The schools must provide a good education; that is, one that is not as harmful as the one offered by the residential schools in the past. Many believe that it is to the advantage of the Canadian government to provide a harmful educational system to First Nations Citizens, one which will eliminate their culture, create dependence, and will not produce leaders capable of interacting with the external political structures.

In Canada the schools are beneficial if they are socialising students well by teaching them to be self-sufficient and functional in the dominant cultural system. It is important to be able to survive in this system, because it is the only place where individuals are allowed to be self-sufficient. The formal educational system is harmful when it takes away the identity of children by weakening the knowledge of their past and culture. These pupils then are no longer stable and productive in either cultural system, because they need those ties that provide them with a sense of personal identity.

The concepts of education seen as "propaganda" and "teaching knowledge" are not opposites. They are more similar than opposites. What would be a beneficial education for one individual could be very harmful for the next individual. The educational system will prove to be beneficial for the individual who is a member of the dominant cultural system. Therefore, the argument that many provide, stating it is Native children and not the educational system that are wrong, since they are offering the same service to non-Indians and First Nations students, is invalid.

Schools for First Nations children are harmful because they are not integrating these children into the dominant cultural system. Schools that Native children attend are not helping them to be "functional." Worse, they are alienating First Nations students from their own culture. The education system alienates the students in the following ways. The children are put in residential schools away from their families and "informal education," and here they are forbidden to speak their Native language and observe their Native rituals. The students are often bussed to school, where they spend four hours a day on a bus, which prevents them from participating in extra-curricular activities. They are almost always taught by "white" teachers, who know little of their heritage; they are not taught subjects objectively. Again, these children are taught a different religion, in a different language, subjected to a different set of expectations. This harm is not felt by the student who is a member of the dominant group, because it is his/her language, religion, and set of expectations.

This section will demonstrate, by using one particular band, how harmful the present educational system is for Native children. The harm arises when teachers of these First Nations students are "white" and know nothing of the myths their pupils have been taught to live by in their informal education. These few pages contain a descriptive analysis of two methods of socialisation employed by the Kwakiutl Indians of British Columbia. These children are educated to understand the important connotations of the menstrual cycle, and regurgitation, myths which teachers know nothing about.

There are many taboos affecting the Kwakiutl woman when she is menstruating. Franz Boaz lists them as follows: she can not go near sick men or newborn children for she will only make them weaker. She can not eat fresh fish, nor can she hunt or fish, not even walk near a river or ocean otherwise the fish will stop flowing. This, they say, is because the animals are repelled by the menstrual blood. She is allowed to pick berries and dig roots. A young girl who is menstruating for the first time is segregated from men and goes through a purifying process. She symbolises the wounded who could bleed to death and when recovering becomes a "life giver."[134]

These myths which the Kwakiutl believe in are functional for their way of life. These taboos would not make sense to the "white European," but, for a band that survives on hunting and gathering, they do. For example, perhaps the taboos forbidding women to hunt and fish were instilled a long time ago to create a natural form of division of labour. The point is that these taboos are logical and operational in the Kwakiutl society.

When stopping to observe these "rules" for the menstruating woman, one can easily recognise that the concepts taught to "white" society are very different from those taught to the Kwakiutl. Therefore, how could a "white" teacher who has not been socialised in the same manner deal with a young girl menstruating for the first time? Or, what consequences would arise from a "white" teacher taking his/her class by a river for a session on nature? And, how would a "white" teacher conduct a class on sex education?

The Kwakiutl are educated to believe that vomiting is a form of recycling and a bridge between one world and another. It plays an important part in their ceremonies. For example, the Hamatsa (Cannibal which also carries the same name as the ceremony), regurgitates all of the flesh he has eaten, because he has been given the power to transform the human flesh into a "creative" substance. For the Kwakiutl the inner being is the connection of two worlds. This explains why everything that is swallowed changes form and emerges either as feces or vomit. The act of vomiting is thus "structurally equivalent to the act of bridging the gaps between the parts of the universe."[135] The act of vomiting is a "homology of death, a magical act, a religious, transcendental, creative act, not merely a physical act."[136]

Again, these beliefs of the Kwakiutl are functional for their way of life. The myths about regurgitation are important to a hunting and gathering band. They associate vomiting with animals, since they observe that wolves and owls do it too. Perhaps the myths of vomiting are closely associated with their respect for nature, perhaps related to a natural system that prevents them from "over-using" their environment. Once more, these myths would have no place in a "white European" circle, but they are important to the Kwakiutl.

The Kwakiutl children are socialised in a formal environment. In their schools, they are taught by a "white" teacher. This person is more often than not unfamiliar with all of the particular nation's myths.[137] The education could be labelled as a bad form of socialisation, because often the teachers believe that their convictions are the correct ones, and they try to persuade the student population that their beliefs are wrong.[138]

Furthermore, the formal and informal educational systems often clash, adding to the confusion of the pupils. Rohner describes an interesting anecdote that relates to informal education. A woman sees children fighting and crying over a tricycle. She acts according to the following belief: "Gertie rewarded the actions of the aggressor-owner. As far as Gertie is concerned, the owner of the tricycle has the right to play with it and he is not expected to share his toys."[139] But when these children enter the formal educational system, they are punished for not sharing their toys with other students. This is only one example of the conflict that exists between the formal and informal education for the Kwakiutl. Rohner elaborates on these inherent contradictions:

> The fact that the life of the children is structured to a very limited extent within the village constitutes another basic discontinuity between the social and cultural background of the children and the expectations of the school. Whereas parents are permissive toward the behaviour of their children, school life is authoritarian and formal. This conflicting situation often imposes as much hardship on the teacher as on the pupils.[140]

There is more than one example of First Nations culture coming into conflict with the formal educational system. Cree children are taught not to make eye contact and that silence is a sign of thoughtfulness and reflection. But "white" teachers demand that students speak up and look them in the eye when they do so. "The children are taught one thing at home, and when they go to school they're taught that it's wrong, Lillian Potts [a councillor and former chief of the Montana band at Hobbema] says. It's a culture shock. The ones who succeed are those who are more adaptable to the dominant society."[141]

The educational system is a propaganda system for the dominant group, because all cultural aspects of the formal education system belong to the dominant group. This in turn denies the cultures of the minority groups and traps them between two cultural systems. This makes the members of minority groups incapable of producing and of breaking the cycle of poverty. The inadequacy in the members of the minority groups, created by the "European" education system, benefits the members of the dominant group. This is why harmful education is often referred to as a propaganda system.

The above examples are extreme; nevertheless, the authorities have recognised the need to have First Nations teachers teach First Nations students. Statistics from 1982-83 demonstrate the fulfilment of this need. However, non-Native teachers outnumber the Cree on-staff teachers by more than two to one in Mistassini. The trend is changing, but it is taking a long time because there are not enough First Nations Citizens who have completed a post-secondary education that would enable them to receive their teaching certificate.

The importance of replacing residential schools with schools in the First Nations communities has been recognised; however, not all communities have their own schools. Of the five communities surveyed in the James Bay area, only one did not have one French and one English elementary school. As of 1982-83 Great Whale had only an English elementary school. Of the five communities, only Mistassini and Great Whale did not have French high schools. Even though all five communities had English secondary schools, not one offered the senior years, secondary IV and V. Great Whale offered only secondary I in English, while Rupert House offered secondary I to III. The other three communities offered only secondary I and II (Table 16). The problem, therefore, has not been resolved. Students wishing to complete high school in English must face long bus rides to the nearest community. But which came first, the high drop-out rates or the lack of availability of senior high school courses? "There is a disastrously high dropout rate among the Hobbema children — beginning as early as Grade 4. By the senior years of high school, the dropout rate is 90 percent."[142]

Even today, the educational system is not what it should be for First Nations children. They are still caught between two ideologies: one that pushes them into a system that is unwilling to accept them, and the other that pushes them into a way of life for which they have no training. Ten months in a classroom does not prepare children for ten months on the traplines. Therefore, the external factor of education is making the Cree of James Bay and other First Nations Citizens dependent on the centre, rendering them unable to support themselves in the city or in the bush.

In summary, the first section of this chapter demonstrated that First Nations Citizens are, in fact, dependent on the centre. Their income is much less than "non-Indians," and their employment rates are also much lower. Many are dependent on government transfer cheques, which provide their major source of income. They are so limited in their economic power that they cannot even provide housing that is not crowded and equipped with a central heating system. The statistics demonstrate that it was not just the isolation factor that influenced these conditions, since "non-Indians" residing near reserves had a higher income, higher employment rate, and better housing conditions. The same tendency was noticed for First Nations Citizens living off reserves and among the general "non-Native" population.

The second section of the chapter determined that violence, suicide, health, and substance abuse are directly influenced by income, housing, and employment of First Nations Citizens. Statistics demonstrated that the levels of violence, suicide, health problems, and substance abuse are much higher for First Nations Citizens. The James Bay Cree and other bands were said to be underdeveloped rather than undeveloped because the human and economic development did not exist, thus explaining their dependence on the centre. If these social problems were not solely caused by the indicators discussed in the section above, then there must be something else influencing these conditions.

The final section of this chapter then made the distinction between external and internal factors that influenced the conditions of First Nations Citizens. It was made clear that both the internal and the external factors influenced the indicators listed above. However, it was stated earlier that the internal factors would not be discussed because of the sensitivity of the subject. Three main points were discussed: the laws, the political climate, and the

Table 16
Education

	Great Whale	Eastmain	Rupert House	Waswanipi	Mistassini
School					
Elementary - Eng.	yes	yes	yes	yes	yes
Elementary - French	no	yes	yes	yes	yes
School					
Secondary - French	no	yes	yes	yes	no
Secondary - English	(1)	(1,2)	(1,2,3)	(1,2)	(1,2)
Teachers On-Staff					
On-Staff - Crees	5	6	12	5	10
On-Staff - Non-Nat.	8	7	18	12	24
Teachers Supply					
On-Staff - Crees	5	11	11	22	24
On-Staff - Non-Nat.	1	1	2	2	3
Pupils Enrolled					
Kindergarten	17	15	57	40	91
Elementary	95	73	247	156	386
Secondary	28	18	75	19	49
Total	140	106	379	215	526
On Staff Teachers per Pupils	10.8	8.2	12.6	12.6	15.5

In 1982-1983; Beaulieu, Denis. *The Crees and Naskapes of Quebec: Their Socio-Economic Conditions.* Direction des Communications du Governement du Québec, 1984, p.40.

educational influence of the dominant culture over human and economic development of First Nations Citizens. The dominant group in this country was found guilty of using many different tactics to assimilate First Nations Citizens, with the intention that one day "Native" issues would disappear. Each failed to make these issues go away, but instead created dependents on the welfare state. Although open racism by the general public was not discussed, it is an important factor that should not be forgotten, since it is often the general public that employs and teaches First Nations Citizens, who suffer from the racism expressed by both the general public and by the institutions. The laws of this country prevent First Nations Citizens from developing economically. The laws take their Indian status away from Native people, and the political institutions take their political powers away from them. Finally, the educational system literally crippled generations of First Nations people, rendering them incapable of functioning in either society, and severely damaging the transmission of their culture.

Instead of eliminating the "Indian" issue, the political institutions gave the "Native" movement a new push. "The modern Native movement emerged in 1969, when the Liberal government of Pierre Trudeau unveiled proposals to abrogate the treaties, repeal the *Indian Act* and transfer responsibility for Indian programs to the provinces."[143] Many have wondered what exactly First Nations people want. If we take the last issue of schools, Thomas Berger states that they want their children to study mathematics, natural sciences, and the other subjects needed for them to be able to function in the dominant society, but they want their children to be able to attend schools where they will not only learn to understand the dominant group but where they will also learn to know themselves.[144] And what do First Nations Citizens want in general? Thomas Berger states that they want to be integrated as a group, rather than individually, into the political, economic, social, and cultural institutions. They do not want to be assimilated, but simply integrated into the dominant society.[145] The demands and desires of First Nations people will be discussed in the conclusion of this book, which will examine the solutions to being marginal, underdeveloped, and being in large part controlled by external forces.

The next chapter, "The Centre Exploiting the Hinterland," will return to concentrating on the James Bay Cree. By using the example of one project, a global view of the domination by the centre will be provided. The James Bay Project is the perfect example of how external forces prevent human and economic development.

Notes

1. Mathews, in Allahar, Anton L. *Sociology and the Periphery: Theories and Issues.* Garamond Press, Toronto, 1989, p.99.
2. York, Geoffrey. *The Dispossessed: Life and Death in Native Canada.* Vintage U.K., London, 1990, pp.4-5.
3. Chance, Norman A. *Summary Report: Developmental Change among the Cree Indians of Quebec*, Rural Development Branch, Ottawa, August, 1970, pp.7-8.
4. Ibid.
5. York, Geoffrey. *The Dispossessed: Life and Death in Native Canada*, p.79.
6. United Nations Development Program. UNDP. *United Nations Development Program World Development Annual Report*, 1990, pp.10-11.
7. Frideres, James S. *Native Peoples in Canada: Contemporary Conflicts.* Prentice-Hall, Scarborough, 1988, p.370.
8. Chance, Norman A. *Summary Report: Developmental Change among the Cree Indians of Quebec*, p.15.
9. Ibid.
10. Indian and Northern Affairs Canada. *Health of Indian Women: Notes on Socio-Demographic Conditions.* Ottawa, 1990, p.30.
11. Frideres, James S. *Native Peoples in Canada: Contemporary Conflicts*, p.164.
12. Ibid.
13. Ibid.
14. Ibid., p.163.
15. Ibid.
16. York, Geoffrey. *The Dispossessed: Life and Death in Native Canada*, pp.2-3
17. Ibid., p.3.
18. Indian and Northern Affairs Canada. *Health of Indian Women: Notes on Socio-Demographic Conditions*, p.30.
19. Frideres, James S. *Native Peoples in Canada: Contemporary Conflicts*, p.169.
20. Ibid.
21. Ibid., p.168.
22. Ibid., p.169.
23. Ibid., pp.168-169.
24. York, Geoffrey. *The Dispossessed: Life and Death in Native Canada*, p.2.
25. Ibid.
26. Ibid., p.72.
27. Ibid., p.73.
28. Ibid., p.74.
29. Ibid., p.73.
30. Frideres, James S. *Native Peoples in Canada: Contemporary Conflicts*, p.370.

31. Indian and Northern Affairs Canada. *Health of Indian Women: Notes on Socio-Demographic Conditions*, p.14.
32. York, Geoffrey. *The Dispossessed: Life and Death in Native Canada*, p.3.
33. Ibid.
34. Ibid., pp.3-4.
35. Ontario Native Womens Association. *Breaking Free: A Proposal for Change to Aboriginal Family Violence*. Thunder Bay, Ontario, December, 1989, p.ii.
36. Ibid.
37. Ibid., p.3.
38. Ibid., p.21.
39. Ibid., p.34.
40. Ibid., p.22.
41. Ibid.
42. York, Geoffrey. *The Dispossessed: Life and Death in Native Canada*, p.28.
43. Ibid., pp.28-29.
44. Indian and Northern Affairs Canada. *Health of Indian Women: Notes on Socio-Demographic Conditions*, p.14.
45. Ibid.
46. Ibid., p.16.
47. Ibid., p.10.
48. United Nations Development Program. UNDP. *United Nations Development Program World Development Annual Report*, p.10.
49. York, Geoffrey. *The Dispossessed: Life and Death in Native Canada*, p.75.
50. Ibid.
51. Ibid., p.68.
52. Indian and Northern Affairs Canada. *Health of Indian Women: Notes on Socio-Demographic Conditions*, p.18.
53. Ibid., p.8.
54. Ibid., p.6.
55. Ibid.
56. York, Geoffrey. *The Dispossessed: Life and Death in Native Canada*, p.78.
57. Ibid., p.79.
58. Ibid.
59. Indian and Northern Affairs Canada. *Supplementary I: Briefing Notes on the James Bay Health Crisis and Epidemic*. Ottawa, 1981, p.1.
60. Ibid.
61. Ibid., p.2.
62. Ibid.
63. Ibid.
64. York, Geoffrey. *The Dispossessed: Life and Death in Native Canada*, p.192.
65. Ibid.
66. Ibid.
67. Ibid.
68. Ibid., p.193.
69. Ibid., p.195.
70. Ibid.
71. Ibid.
72. Ibid., p.8.
73. Ibid., p.9.
74. Ibid.
75. Ibid.
76. Ibid.

77. Ibid., p.10.
78. Ibid.
79. Ibid.
80. Ibid., p.11.
81. Ibid.
82. Ibid.
83. Ibid.
84. Ibid., p.12.
85. Ibid., p.13.
86. Ibid., p.14.
87. Ibid., p.16.
88. Ibid.
89. Ibid., p.18.
90. Ontario Native Womens Association. *Breaking Free: A Proposal for Change to Aboriginal Family Violence*, p.7.
91. Ibid., p.51.
92. Ibid., p.50.
93. York, Geoffrey. *The Dispossessed: Life and Death in Native Canada*, p.146.
94. Ibid.
95. Ibid.
96. Ibid., p.145.
97. Janigan, Mary. "Lonely Cries of Distrust: Anger and Pain Fuel Native Claims." *Maclean's*, vol. 105, no. 11, March 16, 1992:22-24, p.23.
98. York, Geoffrey. *The Dispossessed: Life and Death in Native Canada*, p.58.
99. Ibid., p.59.
100. Ibid.
101. Frideres, James S. *Native Peoples in Canada: Contemporary Conflicts*, p.371.
102. York, Geoffrey. *The Dispossessed: Life and Death in Native Canada*, pp.59-60.
103. Brecher, Irving (ed.). *Human Rights, Development and Foreign Policy: Canadian Perspectives*. The Institute for Research on Public Policy, Halifax, Nova Scotia, 1989, p.98.
104. Ibid.
105. Ibid., pp.98-99.
106. Ibid., p.99.
107. Ibid., p.98.
108. Ibid.
109. Ibid., p.99.
110. Ibid., p.104.
111. Ibid., pp.104-105.
112. Frideres, James S. *Native Peoples in Canada: Contemporary Conflicts*, p.146.
113. Ibid.
114. Ibid.
115. Indian and Northern Affairs Canada. *Health of Indian Women: Notes on Socio-Demographic Conditions*, p.4.
116. Allahar, Anton L. *Sociology and the Periphery: Theories and Issues*, p.92.
117. Janigan, Mary. "Lonely Cries of Distrust: Anger and Pain Fuel Native Claims," p.23.
118. Frideres, James S. *Native Peoples in Canada: Contemporary Conflicts*, p.345.
119. Ibid.
120. York, Geoffrey. *The Dispossessed: Life and Death in Native Canada*, p.59.
121. Ibid.
122. Ibid., p.60.

123. Ibid.
124. Ibid.
125. Frideres, James S. *Native Peoples in Canada: Contemporary Conflicts*, p.370.
126. Ontario Native Womens Association. *Breaking Free: A Proposal for Change to Aboriginal Family Violence*, p.9.
127. Chance, Norman A. *Summary Report: Developmental Change among the Cree Indians of Quebec*, p.13.
128. Ibid.
129. York, Geoffrey. *The Dispossessed: Life and Death in Native Canada*, p.23.
130. Ibid., p.22.
131. Frideres, James S. *Native Peoples in Canada: Contemporary Conflicts*, p.174.
132. York, Geoffrey. *The Dispossessed: Life and Death in Native Canada*, p.37.
133. Ray, Douglas and al. "Lifelong Education: An Emerging Human Right." *Human Rights in Canadian Education*. Kendall/Hunt Publishing Co., Dubuque, Iowa, 1983, p.5.
134. Boaz, Franzn. *Kwakiutl Ethnography*. The University of Chicago Press, Chicago, "1966." (original date unpublished), pp.135-140.
135. Walens, Stanley. *Feasting with Cannibals: An Essay on Kwakiutl Cosmology*. Princeton University Press, 1981, p.62.
136. Ibid.
137. Parnell, Ted. *Barriers to Education*. Yukon Association of Non-Status Indians, Whitehorse, Yukon, 1976, pp.38-40.
138. Ibid.
139. Rohner. "The Kwakiutl: Indians of British Columbia," *Minority Canadians 1 — Native People*, Prentice Hall, Scarborough, Ontario, 1971, p.128.
140. Ibid., p.129.
141. York, Geoffrey. *The Dispossessed: Life and Death in Native Canada*, p.51.
142. Ibid.
143. Janigan, Mary. "Lonely Cries of Distrust: Anger and Pain Fuel Native Claims," p.23.
144. Berger, Thomas R. *Liberté fragile: Droits de la personne et dissidence au Canada*. (1981) Editions Hurtubise HMH Ltée, Ville de la Salle, Québec, 1985, p.258.
145. Ibid., p.63.

Chapter 4

The Centre Exploiting the Hinterland: The James Bay Hydroelectric Project

The James Bay Project is a great example of how a centre can dominate a periphery. In this case, the centre has not only dominated the environment of the Cree, but also their lives. Many of the social problems crippling the Cree, which were discussed in the previous chapter, can be directly linked to the James Bay Project. This chapter will examine the emergence of the Project, the battles fought, and the outcome of James Bay. The information is divided into two sections, each containing four subsections. The first section, entitled "Battles Fought and Lost," will begin with a physical description of the Project, followed by a look at the political motivation of the centre, the opposition that the Project met, and finally the signing of the James Bay and Northern Quebec Agreement. The second section of this chapter, "Damage Done," will begin with a look at the environmental damages, the displacement of towns, the social problems of the Cree, and finally the broken promises of the Québec government.

Sean McCutcheon is the author most often cited in this final chapter, because McCutcheon's book, *Electric Rivers: The Story of the James Bay Project*, is more technical than the other sources consulted. His book is more neutral than other sources, leading me to believe that the data is more impartial. McCutcheon's book also covered all political actions of the provincial and federal governments surrounding the James Bay Project, something which other sources lacked.

Many of the James Bay Cree call the area they live in a garden. Job Bearskin, a Cree hunter, speaks fondly of this land: "this whole place is like a garden, because many things grow here, and the Indians are one of the things that grow here."¹ Bearskin speaks of the great balance between his people and the animals, and the fact that sharing the gifts of nature has always been at the centre of their ways. This chapter will examine what happened to "Job's Garden," the balance between man and animal, and to the sharing.

Battles Fought and Lost

The James Bay Project is a hydroelectric development of great magnitude. It is located in northern Québec and produces electricity by damming the rivers that flow into James Bay. In fact, "the James Bay project, the most expensive energy project in the history of North America, calls for the diversion or alteration of 20 northern rivers though the construction of 36 dams and more than 1,000 dikes."[2] The area of land is difficult to visualise, and so many describe the area in terms of other countries or areas with which they are familiar. For example, Augusta Dwyer states that "when and if completed, after the year 2000, the project will have flooded 23,000 square kilometres of land, [and] irrevocably damaged a wilderness approximately the size of Newfoundland island and Labrador combined."[3]

The James Bay development is made up of three projects. The first project, La Grande, was divided into two phases. La Grande Phase I was completed in 1985. It "dammed five rivers and diverted them into the La Grande River."[4] La Grande "from its headwaters in the highland of the Québec-Labrador Peninsula ... flows some 800 kilometres westward, down to James Bay."[5] However, La Grande is no longer a river but a series of reservoirs and hydroelectric installations. La Grande-2 dam, better known as LG-2, "is as high as a 50-story building."[6] The reservoir at LG-2 took well over a year to fill. Thirteen years after the construction of La Grande Phase I, "more than 10,000 square kilometres of natural waterways and land have been flooded."⁷ There are approximately 206 dykes and nine dams that make up the La Grande Phase I, whose three powerhouses generate 10,282 megawatts.⁸

Construction on La Grande Phase II began in 1986. Its estimated date of completion is sometime in 1996. The main river involved in this phase is the Eastmain. Upon completion, there will be approximately 125 dykes and six dams. The four existing powerhouses and the two future ones will create an output of 4,509 megawatts.⁹

The second project is the Great Whale. It involves the Great Whale River, just north of La Grande. Its scheduled start date was 1992, and contractors estimate it to be completed in the year 2000. This complex "involves the diversion and development of the last of the wild rivers flowing into James Bay and southern Hudson Bay and is the centre of the current controversy."¹⁰ The three powerhouses are expected to generate 3,060 megawatts of power. These powerhouses would be supported by approximately 133 dykes and five dams.¹¹

"The third and final stage, the Nottaway-Broadback-Rupert (NBR) Project, would see work of a similarly lofty scale in the drainage basin of three great rivers flowing into the foot of James Bay."¹² Construction is scheduled to commence in 1995, with no completion date having been estimated. There are approximately 579 dykes and sixteen dams scheduled for construction. The minimum of eleven powerhouses would generate 9,100 megawatts of power upon completion.¹³

Augusta Dwyer states that, once complete, the entire James Bay Project will have "pepper[ed] about 350,000 square kilometres of wilderness — a little more than 20 percent of Canada's largest province — with roads, airports, dams, dykes, reservoirs, powerhouses, and transmission towers."¹⁴ Furthermore, "the entire James Bay project will generate, at peak output some 27,000 megawatts of power, equivalent to the output of 35 or more nuclear power plants. Hydro-Quebec, which now generates a quarter of all the hydroelectricity in North America, will have increased that fraction to two-thirds."[15]

But how do the reservoirs, powerhouses, dams, and dykes work? Electricity is created when the fast flow of water makes the turbines in the powerhouses turn. The stronger the flow of the water, the more power created; therefore, powerhouses are often built downstream from waterfalls or where the river drops. At this point, dams will be built to further increase the height from which the water will fall, hence increasing the force of the water. Each powerhouse is equipped with valves that allow for spillwaters, to prevent the dams from being destroyed by the overflow of the reservoir. "Dams and dikes differ only in function. A dam blocks a river in a massive manifestation of human domination of nature. A dike limits the spread of water raised by a dam."[16] The reservoirs are then formed behind the dams, since when the dams "plug a river," the water will spread. The reservoirs are always upstream from the powerhouses, in order to increase the fall of the water, but they are also constructed upstream to divert rivers and create water supplies that help regulate the production of electricity in time of high demand. Some reservoirs are so large that they can actually accumulate water from one wet year to be used in a dry year.

One way of explaining the size of the James Bay Project is to look at the costs involved. In this case, it was determined that, ultimately, bigger was cheaper. As many Crees have mentioned, however, the cost of the land was not taken into account. The land was regarded as free; therefore, only the costs of the installations and infrastructures were included in the price tag of several billion dollars.

Once the government decided on the construction of La Grande Phase I, it began to build a road to the work site. The plans were to go far north to La Grande, because the river beds in the south could not support the dikes. In June of 1971, the bulldozers moved at a rate of more than one kilometre a day, beginning at Matagami, the most northern point of the road system. They simply tore down the trees and levelled the land, creating a crude road with compact snow as a surface, with the frozen ice acting as bridges. "When the road reached the La Grande-2 site in 1973, trucks began rolling north with bulldozers, fuel, food, and building supplies."[17] By 1977, the north-south road was paved, and there was an "east-west axis, a gravel road which reached the Caniapiscau work site, 725 kilometres to the east...."[18]

The complex was indeed the "largest construction site in the world: 1,000 kilometres from east to west, 200 kilometres from the north to the south."[19] "At the peak of construction, in 1978 and 1979, there were some 20,000 people on the James Bay work sites, and more than 2,000 to the south, building power lines.[20] All the installations were built to accommodate this large work force. There were sports facilities, cinemas, banks, and bars. Once the project was completed, construction crews left behind them "some 1,600 kilometres of roads, five airports, thousands of kilometres of high-voltage power lines, and hundred of millions of cubic meters of dirt, piled into synthetic mountains, the collective product of politicians' schemes, engineers' calculations, and labourers' sweat."[21] There are few power lines belonging to Hydro-Quebec, but since the total length of these lines is so long, Hydro-Quebec's high-voltage transmission network exceeds that of any other utility in the world. The cost of this first phase of La Grande is between sixteen and twenty billion dollars. The estimated cost at the beginning of the project was six billion dollars. This price tag does include the thousands of kilometres of high voltage line, however, and the price of the land is not included.[22]

The James Bay Project has been described from the first to its final stages. Listing the numbers of square kilometres of roads, powerlines, and flooded land gives one a sense of the enormity of the project, but the purpose of this exercise is to demonstrate the dominance of the centre on the periphery. The centre has the power to create this much change and destruction on the Cree.

The following section will discuss the political attitudes of the Québec government which developed this grandiose plan.

Robin Philpot put forth the argument that the underlying conflict is between the French and the English rather than the Cree and the Québec government. These are in fact two nations who are fighting for more control over their destiny. These are two nations that were meant to be assimilated, but who resisted, to the great chagrin of the federal government. It has been a sore point, because the Cree who encountered the English first, speak English rather than French. The Québec government was insulted when the Cree fought them on Bills 178 and 101, which determine the language that Québec residents are to use in school and at work. Both the James Bay Development Corporation and the James Bay Energy Corporation were represented by French speaking lawyers; on the other hand, the lawyers and specialists representing the James Bay Cree in court were English. Perhaps more important, the Cree were traditionally backed by the largest of the English powers, the federal government. One can not reduce this conflict to a simple ongoing fight between the French and the English; the idea of centre and periphery is also very present in this battle.

Sean McCutcheon put forth the argument, in his book *Electric Rivers*, that Hydro-Quebec's hydroelectric project was created in response to domination by English Canada. In the 1930s, Québec realised that it was one of the only places in the world where electricity was privately owned. Once politicians examined the names of the owners and management of these companies, they realised that all were English-speaking. Therefore, two stages of nationalisation were introduced by the Québec government: "in April 1944 it bought, for a handsome sum, Montréal Light, Heat and Power Consolidated and its power-generating subsidiaries, and gave them to a new, publicly owned utility known as Hydro-Quebec."[23] The second stage of nationalisation took place during the Quiet Revolution. René Lévesque had been elected in the 1962 election, which he turned "into a virtual referendum on his proposal to nationalise the remaining private electric utilities in Québec. He won."[24] He borrowed 600 million dollars to buy the remaining privately owned electric companies.[25]

In 1970, Robert Bourassa was elected Premier of Québec. At this point, his ideas on James Bay were already quite clear. In his mind, Québec did not want independence but simply to be strong. He believed the way to achieve more autonomy was through economic means. "If we want to be a proud, strong people," Bourassa said, "it's not with independence we will achieve that goal, it's with economic strength. Where could Québec increase its economic strength? It's with its natural resources, which are almost illimitable. Where could we have those resources? It is in the North."[26] It's not surprising that the leader of the centre would declare the exploitation of the periphery as a means to gain economic strength.

The October Crisis began October 5, 1970, when James Cross was kidnapped by the Front de Libération du Québec (FLQ). Five days later, Pierre Laporte was kidnapped. By October 16, Bourassa asked Pierre Trudeau, the Prime Minister of Canada, to "invoke the War Measures Act, a law by which the federal government could assume sweeping and repressive power in order to put down insurrection."[27] But after these events, according to Sean McCutcheon, Bourassa looked weak, turning to the federal government for help. Bourassa needed something to regain his popularity; therefore, a few months later, on April 30, 1971, he launched the James Bay Project.

The James Bay Development Corporation and the James Bay Energy Corporation were created by Bourassa in July 1971. These government-owned and controlled corporations were created to bypass any opposition from Hydro-Quebec. "Hydro-Quebec, however, was not so easily circumvented. It took over the Energy Corporation, and thus became master of the James Bay project which, it had now decided, should be built."[28]

Hydro-Quebec was over-generous when creating estimates of the growth of demand in electricity in the decades to come. However, the people in charge of borrowing the estimated 6 billion dollars for La Grande were not as generous. They met with politicians and finally agreed to an estimate that was still higher than that of other utilities with similar growth markets. New York State lent an initial 600 million dollars to Hydro-Quebec; the rest has been borrowed on Wall Street. All loans to Hydro-Quebec are guaranteed by the provincial government.

In 1983, Hydro-Quebec reported having a surplus of energy which they could not sell; therefore, they postponed La Grande Phase II until they had increased their sales. Within the next three years, they signed contracts with at least four utility companies in New England. The United States signed with Hydro-Quebec because it was the cheapest seller: the cost was equivalent to just "80 percent of the cost of the electricity generated at oil or coal-fired plants in the United States."[29] But something began to happen to Hydro-Quebec. At first they exported electricity because they had a surplus, but now they wanted to create surpluses in order to export. Hydro-Quebec is selling its electricity to the Green Mountain Power Corporation, "a member of the Vermont Joint Owners Consortium ... buying power from Québec for 30 percent below its next-cheapest supply alternative."[30] And yet Hydro-Quebec will borrow more money to pay for phase II of James Bay than any other company in Canada. Even though Hydro-Quebec produces power to export rather than to supply the energy needs of its population, creditors continue to lend money to Hydro-Quebec because its revenue of six billion dollars last year was enough to cover the overhead and the interest on its loans.

Québec's philosophy throughout this debate has been to meet the needs of the majority, regardless of the harm done to the minority. Leaders have used the following argument as a means to justify the environmental damages. Bourassa states: "You don't have to be a Nobel prize winner to know that a hydro plant protects the environment better than a coal-fired or a nuclear plant. To be convinced of that, you just have to go to Three Mile Island or Chernobyl."[31] Meanwhile, the federal government has refused to get involved, when the only thing at stake is the James Bay environment and the mental and physical health of the Cree. "Ottawa wants to avoid antagonising Québec, with which it is engaged in yet another round of negotiations as to how powers should be divided within Canada, and nothing would antagonise Québec more than a confrontation over hydro-electric projects, the symbol and seat of economic power in the province."[32]

As the instigator of the James Bay Project has said, the needs of the majority are more important. As it happens, the majority are in the centre, not the periphery. One can not state that the conflict is simply between the French and the English on this issue; it's between two nations fighting for control, and between the centre and the periphery as well. As many First Nations Citizens have said, the only way to hurt a white man is through his wallet.

What were the Cree doing while the politicians were determining their fate? They were fighting a losing battle. It all began with newspaper articles published in the "south." Bourassa had just declared that "we must conquer the North."[33] Crees learned through the day-old newspapers of Bourassa's plan to construct the James Bay Project. They were never consulted, even though it would be their traplines that were going to be flooded. Phillip Awashish, "one of the first generation Cree to have completed secondary school," had a meeting in his home in June 1971, shortly after Bourassa launched the James Bay Project.[34] This meeting reunited, for the first time, representatives of the eight Cree communities of the region. Since they had no political structures of their own, they united under the Indians of Quebec Association. After their meeting, the Crees drafted a resolution: "We, the representatives of the Cree bands that will be affected by the James Bay hydro project or any other project, oppose to these projects [sic] because we believe that only the beavers had the right to build dams in our territory."[35]

It was also at this time that Trudeau was taking steps to shift the responsibility for First Nations Citizens to the provinces. Not wanting to get involved, the federal government simply gave the Indians of Quebec Association half a million dollars to fight the James Bay Project. Both Phillip Awashish and Billy Diamond, chief of Waskaganish, the village at the mouth of the Rupert River, began hiring experts, mainly recruited from McGill University. The Crees took the case to court, not because they were rejecting progress, but because they wanted some control over the land on which they were dependent. James O'Reilly, one of the legal advisors of the Cree and Inuit, suggested that they petition the Supreme Court of Canada to stop construction at the James Bay site until further research was done, because the work was irreversible.

In November 1972, hearings began with Judge Albert Malouf presiding. The case made by Hydro-Quebec, the James Bay Development Corporation, and the Energy Corporation did not begin until March 1973. The defence argued that the Cree were dependent on store-bought food, unemployment, government transfers, and welfare; therefore, they had already given up their traditional way of life. In this argument, Hydro-Quebec is actually confirming the fact that when the periphery depends on the centre it destroys the culture. They also stated that "halting the construction would inconvenience all the people of Québec, who would need more electricity; since there were far more Quebecers than Natives, the interests of the majority should prevail over those of the minority."[36] The defence claimed that the Cree had already given up their traditional way of life when they purchased "skidoos, and houses with electricity, refrigerators, radios, beds, dishes, and even telephones."[37] An anthropologist for the defence told the court that a shock to a culture was always good since a culture should never be stagnant. The defence told the court that the average income of Fort George Crees, for the previous year, was $10,167. Many accepted these figures, which included all funding given by the federal and provincial governments for infrastructures, such as roads and municipal buildings. Experts for the defence claimed that only 1.85 percent of the James Bay area was to be flooded and that this flooding was in fact good for the land. According to Mr. Justice Turgeon, "there is no proof that the management of the James Bay territory will not render the ecological modifications beneficial as a whole."[38]

On November 15, 1973, Justice Malouf rendered his verdict in favour of the Cree and Inuit. He ordered Hydro-Quebec, the James Bay Development Corporation, the James Bay Energy Corporation, and twenty-two independent contractors as follows:

> (a) to immediately cease, desist, and refrain from carrying out works, operations, and projects in the territory described in the schedule of Bill 50, including the building of roads, dams, dykes, bridges, and connected works.
>
> (b) to cease, desist, and refrain from interfering in any way with petitioners' rights, from trespassing in the said territory and from causing damage to the environment and the natural resources of the said territory.[39]

After his five months of deliberation, Justice Malouf recognised the fact that the Cree and the Inuit were in fact dependent on the land, and, furthermore, that the condition of the land had direct effects on living conditions and culture. Despite the ruling, the James Bay Project continued to evolve in a sealed area. All helicopter pilots wanting to bring any media personnel into the sealed area were threatened with having their licenses revoked. "The day after the Malouf judgement, the corporation entered two appeals to the Quebec Court of Appeals. One was against the merits of the Malouf judgement, and one was an application that the effect of the Malouf judgement should be suspended pending hearing, at a later date, of the appeal."[40] Exactly a week after Malouf's ruling, the Quebec Court of Appeals overturned a decision that had taken seventy-eight days of hearings and five months of deliberation to reach. When it came time for the Crees and Inuit to appeal the latest decision by the Quebec Court of Appeals, they had to wait eight months as opposed to a week. Meanwhile, the construction of the James Bay Project continued.

Bourassa was anxious to settle out of court, since the investors were worried about a possible impasse. The Premier made an offer of "among other things, payment of $100-million."[41] The Cree families, having been flown out of the bush, voted "no" to the proposal in March 1974. "The Indian lands are not for sale, not for millions and millions of dollars," said Billy Diamond.[42] Meanwhile, the Indians of Quebec Association was replaced by the Grand Council of the Cree (of Québec), with Billy Diamond as the Grand Chief, and the Northern Quebec Inuit Association, with Charlie Watts as a leader and founder. While the negotiations were continuing between these associations and the provincial government, so was the construction of the hydroelectric project. The Cree and Inuit felt that the more the work progressed and money poured into the project, the lower their chances to stop the James Bay Project from becoming a reality. They decided to settle out of court, but only after Mr. Chrétien threatened to cut all funds to the Cree and Inuit if they did not settle — funds that were earmarked to appeal their land claims. Their demands were the following:

> The Crees wanted, above all, to preserve their traditional life style ... and so they were bargaining for land to be set aside on which only Crees could hunt, trap, and fish. As well, they wanted as much autonomy as they could get. For instance, they wanted to take over the administration of the hospi-

tals, schools, and other institutions serving their communities from distant, paternalistic, non-Native bureaucrats. They wanted procedures to protect the environment, and a say in development in the James Bay region. And they wanted money in compensation for what they would give.[43]

Finally, after a year and eight months of negotiations, the 455 page document was signed. Other First Nations Citizens across the country accused the Cree and Inuit of selling-out.

In November of 1975, the James Bay Northern Quebec Agreement was signed, offering, including the amendments, a total of 500 million dollars, 75 percent of which was to go to the Cree over a 20 year period.[44] Under the agreement, the land north of the 49th parallel, or two-thirds of the province, is divided into four categories. The first Category IA, consists of 1,274 square miles of land to be used by the Cree and 3,130 square miles by the Inuit. This land surrounds the existing communities and is to be retained by the Québec government but administered by the federal government. The land for the Inuit is "held by Inuit municipal corporations."[45] Category IB is 884 square miles of land "designated to be owned by the Cree communities. These lands are to be alienated only to the province, which can expropriate, but must pay compensation. Mineral rights are to be retained by the province, but their development is dependent on the consent of Cree authorities."[46] The third section, Category II land is 28,130 square miles for the Cree and 35,000 square miles for the Inuit, on which only these First Nations may hunt. The province has the right to use this land in any manner without consent and without obligation of compensation. Non-Natives may enter this area for any other reason but hunting. The final category, Category III, "the rest of the lands of northern Québec — 350,000 square miles — are surrendered by the Native people, and are available to the province for development."[47] (See Table17.)

Table 17
Land Divisions Under the James Bay and Northern Agreement

Category	KM²	Hunting	Title of the Land	Administration Management, and Control	Development and Expropriation
CATEGORY (1A)					
Cree	1,274	exclusive to First Nations	provincial Inuit Municipal corporation	Municipal* Government	Mineral Rights are held by the Province
Inuit	3,130				Province may develop land with compensation
(1B)	884	exclusive to First Nations	Cree communities alienable only to the province	Federal government	Crees must approve development
CATEGORY (11)					Province may develop land without consent and without compensation**
Cree	28,130	exclusive to First Nations	provincial government	provincial government	
Inuit	35,000				
CATEGORY (111)	350,000	open to "whites" under the provincial government	provincial government	provincial government	provincial government

*"In 1978, 420 Naskapi living near Schefferville were, in effect, written into the James Bay and Northern Quebec Agreement, and in 1984 the Canadian government passed the *Cree-Naskapi (of Québec) Act*, establishing a municipal form of government covering the Category 1A lands. This Act replaces the *Indian Act*, and removes the Crees and Naskapi from the direct control of the federal Minister of Indian Affairs." Richardson, Boyce. *Strangers Devour the Land.* Vancouver: Douglas & McIntyre Ltd., 1991, pp.323-324.

** All non-Natives are allowed on the Category 11 lands. They are permitted to do research, development, and all other activities, except for hunting.

Data compiled from Boyce Richardson's text. Richardson, Boyce. *Strangers Devour the Land.* Vancouver: Douglas & McIntyre Ltd., 1991, pp.323-324.

Over twelve committees, boards, and corporations were funded to manage the responsibility allocated by the James Bay Agreement. Corporations were funded to control the economic development of the James Bay area, while boards and committees, many containing representatives of the federal government, "assumed control of school boards, health and social service boards, and municipal services, for which the federal and provincial governments would pay."[48] Another important settlement that was made in the agreement was the *Hunters and Trappers Income Security Program*. This program enables the Cree and Inuit to continue to make a living in their traditional ways while receiving 11,000 dollars a year; the amount varies, among other things according to the number of days spent hunting and trapping. Hence, this program promotes the traditional way of life by allowing the Cree and Inuit to sustain themselves by hunting, regardless of the international fur industry.

The court appearances and negotiations surrounding the James Bay Project have "triggered a Quiet Revolution among the Natives in Northern Québec — a period marked by rapid modernisation, the creation of nation-building bureaucracies, national affirmation, and the politics of victimisation."[49] They have taken charge of the education of their children and their cultural survival by instating programs, one of which stipulates that during the first three years of their education, children will be taught in their mother tongue. They have also understood that much of their strength lies in economic independence; therefore, they are investing in their own airlines and construction companies. Furthermore, they have seen the damage done by La Grande and are now fighting the construction of Great Whale. Mathiew Coon-Come, elected Grand Chief in 1987, speaks for the Cree: "Why spend billions of dollars to destroy the environment and to destroy my people just to export electricity to the United States? Does this make any sense? We are fighting for our survival. Aboriginal nations have been pushed aside for too long. The problem with Bourassa's dream is that it is fast becoming an environmental and economic nightmare."[50] As Quebecers were fighting for separatism during the Quiet Revolution, the Cree nation is fighting against James Bay II and III.

The Cree are working hard to get the Great Whale Project stopped. This time they may succeed. Their circumstances have changed in their favour in the past twenty years. Since 1975, the environmental movement has increased on a global level, raising the ecological consciousness of most. Quebecers are much more concerned about the provincial debt and have seen that the final cost of Phase I was more than double the initial estimates. They have noticed that the promised jobs were only temporary ones, and they have seen the value of their homes decrease, without compensation, due to the high-voltage power lines crossing to the United States. The government of the United States has noticed that its constituents resent the fact that importing electricity from Québec takes jobs away from American competitors in this recession/depression. During the last decade, the Cree have become accustomed to fighting the government, and they have changed their direction in order to gain public support. They talk less of cultural genocide and more of the environment and the global effects of the James Bay Project, as well as cost and efficiency. Their campaign had them canoe all the way to New York city for Earth Day. The Cree have tried to get the utility companies to cancel their contracts with Hydro-Quebec. If Hydro-Quebec has nowhere to sell its surplus power, it could not justify spending billions of dollars to create more. They have succeeded in getting companies in Vermont, New York, and Maine to cancel their contracts. However, much of the battle is over the James Bay and Northern Agreement. Québec states that the Cree and Inuit gave up all rights to the land when they signed the Agreement, but these First Nations still claim a right of say over the development of the area.

This concludes the first section of this chapter, where the manner in which the centre uses the raw resources of the hinterland for its own benefit has been examined. The Cree remain dependent on the centre, since they can not exploit their own resources. They are given some compensation in terms of money, but none of the promised jobs with Hydro-Quebec, since they lack the qualifications and do not speak French. Perhaps the Cree would not oppose the James Bay Project so vigorously if only they had benefitted from the construction. As things stand, they only have been "inconvenienced." The following section will examine what the James Bay Project has also created, besides producing electricity. These issues include damage to the environment, displacement of towns, the creation of social problems, and a constant fight by the Cree to obtain what the provincial government promised in the James Bay and Northern Agreement.

Damage Done

Some Cree have seen their traplines completely or partially flooded, while others now have major highways running through their hunting grounds. This has meant, among other things, a redistribution of the traplines among the hunting families, disrupting a division that had existed for centuries. But they had already gone through this change under the command of the Hudson's Bay Company. Many of their campsites and graves are now submerged. Rivers where fishermen would fish have become reservoirs, dried out, or have been diverted. The birds have disappeared after having their feeding grounds altered. The calving grounds of the beluga whales are affected with the sudden increase of fresh water into the salt water of the Hudson Strait. The changes to the environment surrounding the Cree are enormous.

The fish are affected in more ways than one. The construction of the James Bay Project has altered the temperature, depth, food supply, and spawning area of the rivers on which the fish depend. One of the best places to fish, the first rapids on La

Grande River, has been replaced by LG-2. But perhaps the most important change in the fish population has been the high increase in mercury poisoning. This is important because mercury poisoning works its way up the food chain; therefore, even if the Cree do not eat the fish in the reservoir which are deemed unsafe, they will be affected if they eat any meat from the surrounding area. The mercury has also spread through rain and snowfall. "Tests on Chisasibi residents in 1984 found high levels of mercury in 64 percent of the population, and some of the elders exhibited the shakiness, numb limbs and loss of peripheral vision of what they call nimassaksiwin, or fish disease."[51] Mercury poisoning is caused by the flooding of the land. Construction crews do not clear the land first "and, bacteria from the drowned, decomposing vegetation transform the insoluble mercury in the rocks into methylmercury."[52] "Though in a stable lake this mercury is broken down by other bacteria, in a new reservoir it is produced more rapidly than breakdown can occur."[53] When Hydro-Quebec began flooding the land, they were aware of mercury poisoning, but they said the methylmercury would return to normal levels after six years. They changed this estimate to thirty years after seeing that the levels were not decreasing; however, independent specialists report that it will take 100 years.[54] "Methylmercury can irreversibly damage the nervous system and brain … Women who ate mercury-contaminated seafood from industrially-polluted Minamata Bay in Japan gave birth to severely damaged children."[55] Because of these severe physical effects, especially on elders, children, and expecting mothers, the Cree can no longer fish in reservoirs or downstream. Fish accounts for a quarter of their food supply. "The proportion of samples of Chisasibi Crees with unacceptable levels rose from about a third in 1977 to two-thirds in 1984."[56] The Mercury Agreement was signed between the Cree and Hydro-Quebec in 1986. The agreement states that 18.5 billion dollars are to be set aside for research and to indicate the lakes and the kinds of fish that have the lowest levels of mercury. This program has helped decrease the levels of mercury found among the Cree.[57]

The caribou were also directly affected by the James Bay Project. First, their calving grounds were flooded. Hydro-Quebec scientists were aware of this, but simply believed that the females would find new grounds. In 1984, the largest herd of caribou, the George River herd, was estimated at more than 600,000 head.[58] In September of 1984, after three years during which the Caniapiscau reservoir was filling, the caribou were making their annual crossing downstream, heading north for the winter. The heavy rains and the spill from the reservoir caused the river to rise so high that almost all of the 10,000 caribou attempting the crossing drowned that year. But, as Hydro-Quebec points out, the deaths are minimal, since there is not one species that is about to be extinct.

The erosion of the shorelines, the flooding of the wetlands, and the deaths in the uplands have forced Hydro-Quebec to spend money on the environment. To appease the people with an environmental conscience, the James Bay Corporation was one of the first Canadian companies, and the first in Québec, to have an environmental department.[59] The James Bay Corporation was pressured into "rehabilitating" the environment of the Cree. They created fishing reservoirs, spawning grounds in designated zones, built docks, and removed some of the dead wood. "They congratulate themselves on being model corporate citizens; no project of this magnitude, they claim, has ever been built with so much respect and care for the environment. During the decade 1974-1984, the Energy Corporation spent $250 million ... on environmental studies."[60]

The Cree have noticed that "there are fewer and fewer geese and ducks each year; the climate is changing; animals are confused because their migration routes have been disrupted; the La Grande is dead."[61] However, the damage would be even greater if Phase III of the James Bay Project were to proceed. The water flooded by the Nottaway, Broadback, and Rupert Rivers would cover twice the area of La Grande. Because the NBR is south of Great Whale and La Grande, the forest and animal life is more abundant; hence, more animals' lives would be directly affected. Since the forest is more dense, the levels of mercury would be even greater in these southern reservoirs than in the north. The drowning of more trees would also add to the global warming through the greenhouse effect, because not only are these trees no longer creating oxygen but "when drowned trees rot under water, they release both carbon dioxide and methane, a potent greenhouse gas."[62] More important than all this reported damage, however, is the unknown damage which still needs to be discovered.

In addition to the environmental damage of the James Bay construction, there has also been a lot of harm done to the inhabitants of the region. "The James Bay Project has disrupted the lives of Native peoples by physically changing their communities and the forests, rivers, and lakes they use, and indirectly, by triggering political rearrangements between Native and non-Native society."[63] Part of this harm also comes from displacing and restructuring the villages. The Cree who have been most affected by the James Bay Project are those from Chisasibi, Great Whale, and Mistassini. When the James Bay and Northern Agreement was signed, Mistassini, being the only Cree village connected to the road system before La Grande was completed, was invaded by "Moonies, kitchenware salesmen, Kung Fu instructors, dope dealers, social scientists, journalists, and others."[64] The Cree of Mistassini felt used, in that they never received any benefits from the long interviews they granted to various media and experts. It has now evolved to "the point where 'only where we see that we can benefit directly, we'll agree to answer questions,' Coon-Come told me ... If I wanted to learn about the social impacts of the James Bay Project, I should read what others had written."[65] The next village to be invaded in the same manner was Great Whale.

People began to pour into Great Whale once the construction of the Great Whale project was announced.

The village that was most affected by the James Bay Project was Chisasibi or Fort George. "Its people lost more of their hunting and trapping lands than did any other Cree community: six of the 40 traplines on which they hunted and trapped are inundated, and many others were partly flooded."[66] The flooding has made small game scarce and poisoned the rivers and reservoirs with mercury. These Cree were fairly isolated on their island, Governor's Island, in the middle of La Grande, but when the flow of their river was increased ten times, their schools, churches, stores, and homes were moved to the mainland. There is currently even talk of relocating the Chisasibi even further inland because scientists had not predicted that the land would erode so quickly. The Chisasibi Cree accepted the Corporation's proposal of funding the construction of a new village on the mainland. A total of 110 million dollars was spent to reach this goal, and the move was completed in 1980.[67]

"Nevertheless, the impact of the James Bay hydro project on the people of Fort George-Chisasibi has been immense. The arrival in their region of up to twenty thousand workers to build the project, with all the amenities needed to sustain them, was a shock. From the beginning, liquor was a problem…[68] As the roads have brought "progress" to the north, the roads have also brought the problems of the south. As the price of commodities has decreased due to the more accessible transportation, so has the cost of alcohol and drugs. "There was a sudden influx of money during the construction boom, as the new town was built. It is connected by road to the La Grande-2 construction site. Though the authorities in both communities tried to limit contact, LG-2 has become a conveniently close source of alcohol and drugs."[69] The other problems often associated with substance abuse have consequently appeared in Chisasibi and the other Cree communities, including family violence. In addition, "the incidence of teenage pregnancies and sexually transmitted diseases is high. The death rate among adolescents and young adults has increased sharply due to accidents, homicides, and suicides, most related to alcohol abuse."[70] The rapid change in northern villages has created social decay and an increase in health problems. Although the levels of tuberculosis have decreased due to the new municipal services, many health problems still exist. Many of the children have cavities, there are high rates of diabetes, and many people suffer from obesity. These health problems did not exist before the 1980s. Many of these health conditions can be related to substance abuse and poor eating habits. However, the underlying cause lies in the change from a traditional way of life. The Cree were never fat, even though they always ate a lot of animal fat, because their modes of transportation were their form of exercise. "They eat less fish than before, for fear of mercury poisoning, and more store-bought foods — those rich in fat, sugar, and carbohydrates, including junk food and candy, are popular."[71] In other words, all of the social ills discussed in the previous chapter of this book can be found in these communities in northern Québec.

Another new problem caused by the flooding created by the James Bay Project has been the fighting between the Cree for hunting land, when their traditional traplines were submerged. The Cree hunters are also fighting with non-Native hunters who have invaded their hunting grounds via the new roads. The traditional way of life is quickly disappearing: "Crees talk with respect about how experienced hunters, by reading subtle signs in nature, can predict such things as when the river ice is safe for travel, when the spring thaw will come, how good the summer fishing will be. But by making the flow regime artificial, the hydroelectric project makes these skills obsolete."[72]

Many of the young men have replaced their hunting traditions with alcohol. Some of the solutions to this problem must come from within the communities, and many efforts are being made. For example, Chisasibi set up a road block in 1989, on the road leading into the village, where all alcohol is confiscated. Since then, the Sûreté du Québec have notified the first woman chief of Chisasibi, Violet Pachanos, that their actions are illegal, since the road is on Category III land. However, the road block continues until the Sûreté du Québec take action to dismantle it, since this initiative has proven effective in lowering the rate of alcohol in the village. Many programs have been set up by outsiders to try to "help" the Cree, but these programs constantly fail, because the Cree are not consulted and do not administer them.

Many experts say that the Cree and other First Nations Citizens are suffering from acculturative stress, a feeling of being caught between two cultures. When individuals attempt to integrate themselves to the dominant group, they are suddenly taken over by strong feelings of guilt. William of Chisasibi finally quit his job at Hydro-Quebec, after almost ten years, because it had driven him to drink. "I was a meter reader," he recalls, "collecting bills and cutting people off when they couldn't pay up. I felt caught in the middle. On the one hand, I wanted to be a good company man, to work nine to five and be on time like the white man. But the Native side of me came into conflict with that because I saw what Hydro-Quebec was doing, how people were being taken advantage of."[73] William solved his inner conflict by moving back to Governor's Island with his wife and dedicating his efforts to stopping Great Whale. Acculturative stress was not part of the agreement, and nor were the other problems discussed here, but, nonetheless, they are present. "We want the best of both worlds, the traditional and the modern," James Bobbish, former chief of Chisasibi, told me, "but what we experience is the worst of both worlds."[74]

The question remains of who really pays and who benefits from the actions of the centre. With all the social and environmental damage, it appears that the Cree are paying for James Bay with their lives and culture, while only the elites rake in the benefits. "Throughout the country," said Billy Diamond, "the Indian people have been the social casualties of development projects. I have seen it out in the west, towns booming, but the Indians poor, gone in prostitution and booze."[75]

Aside from fighting the Corporations against the construction of Great Whale, the Cree are also fighting in the courts to have the conditions found in the James Bay and Northern Agreement upheld. "Perhaps the worst instance of the government's unwillingness to abide by the agreement came in 1981, when eight Cree children died of diarrhea. The cause was determined to be the open sewers left in many partially reconstructed Cree villages after government money for completing the sewage system was cut off."[76] Eighty more of these children were hospitalised in the James Bay area for the same symptoms.[77] Ever since then, those who promised the money in the James Bay Agreement have been dragged into court to pay what was agreed upon for the hospitals, schools, and other infrastructures.

"Their chief lawyer, James O'Reilly, has calculated that because of these broken promises the Crees are already owed 1 billion dollars. They are angered at talks of money for accepting James Bay II. What they want is to own and control the land and all its resources, including the rivers that Hydro-Quebec, without their consent, is exploiting."[78] The Corporations are tired of hearing the Cree cry "genocide and environmental disaster," since they believe this is a ploy used to get more money out of the next agreement. The Cree claim that the James Bay Agreement was signed only for the first and second stages of La Grande and not for the Great Whale and the Nottaway, Broadback, and Rupert developments. After all they have seen of the damage and extent of the impact of the James Bay Project on the area, many of the Cree who signed the agreement in 1974 said that they would never do it again.

The corporations argue that they have a right to build the Great Whale and Nottaway, Broadback, and Rupert Projects, since this land was in the agreement. However, the Cree are fighting this decision in court, and they believe that they have fundamental rights to the land, and that they are not being consulted on the development of the James Bay region, something which was very specific in the agreement. The Corporations are using every trick they know to have the Great Whale Project move forward. When they were told by the courts that they could not proceed until more recent environmental studies could be done, they divided the project into two. They then submitted a proposal for the first phase, which consisted in setting up all infrastructures needed to complete the Great Whale Project. However, Cree activists won a small battle when the Québec government announced that it would postpone James Bay II for at least a year.

In conclusion, the Cree are telling the world that not only are they not receiving any benefits from the hydroelectric project, which has only caused them pain, but that the south is not even being careful about the way in which they spend the megawatts. "Quebecers use more electricity per person (and more electricity per unit of economic value produced) than almost any other people in the world."[79] Because the hydro is so cheap, many companies and individuals "waste it."[80] The companies in the United States pay much more for their electricity, and hence they are spending more and more money on installing and researching energy efficient products. "Energy analyst Amory Lovins has coined the term 'negawatts' for the units of electricity power which, because they were saved, the utility did not have to generate."[81] The "negawatts" are created by using such products as energy-efficient lightbulbs, insulation, doors, refrigerators, windows, toilettes, and shower heads, to name a few. "According to Lovins, in the 1980s, the United Sates has been getting seven times more new energy from savings as from net increases in supply."[82]

Environmental activists and the Cree are promoting the benefits of "negawatts." They have determined that it is cheaper for Hydro-Quebec to create "negawatts" than electricity; furthermore, that it is cheaper for the companies in the United States to create "negawatts" than it is to import electricity from Québec. Not only does it cost less, but it also stimulates the economy. "In Québec, demand side measures programs create about four times more jobs per dollar than do investments in hydroelectric dams."[83] Several sectors benefit from these job opportunities, and more jobs requiring lower skills are needed when creating "negawatts" than when operating the James Bay Projects. "Finally, efficiency programs do negligible damage to the environment."[84] Hydro-Quebec has been pressured to invest in conservation measures. They plan on spending 2 billion dollars in the next decade on conservation.[85] However, Hydro-Quebec and the politicians claim that they cannot save enough to warrant them not building the final phases of James Bay.

"Hydro-Quebec's critics say its conservation efforts are puny; less than the other two major electric utilities in Canada, Ontario Hydro and B.C. Hydro, and a good deal less than many American utilities. Hydro-Quebec is only spending on conservation about one-twentieth of what it is spending on dams."[86] Many believe that the small conservation efforts "are designed to free power for export sales, not to reduce power generation."[87] As discussed earlier in this chapter, much of the inertia of the James Bay Project comes from the politicians who use it in their election campaigns.

Bourassa and other politicians believe that they are in fact helping Québec's economy, but, instead, they are creating a Third World nation state. One of the fundamental characteristics of an undeveloped nation is that its major source of income is derived from natural resources. "Hydro-Quebec has grossly over-invested and, in order to repay its mounting debt, was caught in a vicious circle, constrained to borrow, build, and sell ever more power at ridiculously cheap rates. Bourassa was turning Québec into an economically dependent Third World nation."[88]

Meanwhile, what happens to the Cree? Well as the corporations and governments have often suggested, the needs of the many far outweigh the "inconveniences" of the few. The Cree are a nation within a nation which is becoming more and more dependent; hence, they are feeling the effects of Québec's condition more and more. The Cree have long been used as a periphery by the centre, but when the centre itself is becoming more and more a periphery, what happens to the Cree? They are bullied into signing the James Bay and Northern Agreement which takes away all their rights, in order to exploit the natural resources found on the land which they claim as their own. This is a complex problem with many factors. In the conclusion of this book, the possible solutions to this situation will be discussed.

Notes

1. Richardson, Boyce. *Strangers Devour the Land*. Douglas and McIntyre Ltd., Vancouver, 1991, p.151.
2. Dwyer, Augusta. "The Trouble of Great Whale," *Equinox*, no. 61, February, 1992:28-41, pp.29-30.
3. Ibid., p.30.
4. Ibid., p.32.
5. McCutcheon, Sean. *Electric Rivers: The Story of the James Bay Project*, Black Rose Books, Montréal, 1991, p.2.
6. Ibid.
7. Ibid., p.3.
8. Dwyer, Augusta. "The Trouble of Great Whale," p.52.
9. Ibid., p.32.
10. Ibid.
11. Ibid.
12. Ibid.
13. Ibid.
14. Ibid.
15. McCutcheon, Sean. *Electric Rivers: The Story of the James Bay Project*, p.4.
16. Ibid., p.65.
17. Ibid., p.70.
18. Ibid., p.73.
19. Ibid.
20. Ibid., p.76.
21. Ibid., p.78.
22. Ibid.
23. Ibid., p.16.
24. Ibid., p.17.

25. Ibid.
26. Ibid., p.30.
27. Ibid., p.32.
28. Ibid., pp.34-35.
29. Ibid., p.84.
30. Ibid., p.142.
31. Ibid., p.147.
32. Ibid., p.181.
33. Ibid., p.42.
34. Ibid.
35. Ibid., p.43.
36. Ibid., p.52.
37. Richardson, Boyce. *Strangers Devour the Land*, p.313.
38. Ibid., p.316.
39. Ibid., p.296.
40. Ibid., p.300.
41. McCutcheon, Sean. *Electric Rivers: The Story of the James Bay Project*, p.55.
42. Ibid.
43. Ibid., p.57.
44. Ibid., p.59.
45. Richardson, Boyce. *Strangers Devour the Land*, p.323.
46. Ibid.
47. Ibid., p.324.
48. McCutcheon, Sean. *Electric Rivers: The Story of the James Bay Project*, p.59.
49. Ibid., p.123.
50. Ibid., p.153.
51. Dwyer, Augusta. "The Trouble of Great Whale," p.38.
52. Ibid.
53. Richardson, Boyce. *Strangers Devour the Land*, p.345.
54. Dwyer, Augusta. "The Trouble of Great Whale," p.38.
55. McCutcheon, Sean. *Electric Rivers: The Story of the James Bay Project*, p.110.
56. Ibid.
57. Ibid., p.111.
58. Ibid., p.104.
59. Ibid., p.97.
60. Ibid., pp.111-112.
61. Ibid., p.112.
62. Ibid., p.164.
63. Ibid., p.117.
64. Ibid.
65. Ibid.
66. Ibid.
67. Richardson, Boyce. *Strangers Devour the Land*, p.342.
68. Ibid., p.340.
69. McCutcheon, Sean. *Electric Rivers: The Story of the James Bay Project*, pp.117-118.
70. Ibid., p.121.
71. Ibid.
72. Ibid., p.119.
73. Dwyer, Augusta. "The Trouble of Great Whale," p.36.
74. McCutcheon, Sean. *Electric Rivers: The Story of the James Bay Project*, pp.121-122.

75. Richardson, Boyce. *Strangers Devour the Land*, p.104.
76. Dwyer, Augusta. "The Trouble of Great Whale," p.36.
77. McCutcheon, Sean. *Electric Rivers: The Story of the James Bay Project*, p.129.
78. Ibid., p.255.
79. Ibid., p.170.
80. Ibid.
81. Ibid., p.171.
82. Ibid.
83. Ibid.
84. Ibid., p.172.
85. Ibid.
86. Ibid., p.173.
87. Richardson, Boyce. *Strangers Devour the Land*, p.355.
88. McCutcheon, Sean. *Electric Rivers: The Story of the James Bay Project*, p.158.

Conclusion

Solutions

This conclusion begins with a brief summary of the main line of thought of each chapter of this book, followed by a discussion of possible solutions to the crisis of First Nations Citizens. The first chapter was devoted to the definition of the dependency theory. This theory, usually applied to Third World countries, was applied to the situation of the Cree of James Bay. There are two main actors in the theory: the centre and the periphery. The centre dominates the periphery by exploiting its non-renewable resources. The peripheries are defined as being dependent on the centre, as having very little control over their own destiny. This dependency was found to be created by both external and internal forces.

The second chapter demonstrated how the Cree of the James Bay region became dependent on the centre, thereby becoming a periphery. The history of the first contact with Europeans tells the story of how the Native's natural resources were surrendered little by little. Much of their land was invaded through treaties, and even more territory was lost without any formal agreements between whites and the Cree.

Once having demonstrated how a nation can become dependent on the centre, it was important to discuss the effects of this dependence on the Cree. However, in the third chapter it was more appropriate to discuss the effects of dependency on all First Nation Citizens in Canada as opposed to just one nation, illuminating the universality of the problem. With the help of statistics, the severity of the problems relating to employment, income, health, and welfare were described.

The fourth and final chapter of this book dealt with the Cree of the James Bay area. This chapter demonstrated how one project directed by the centre can destroy the citizens of the periphery. The James Bay Project is responsible for the destruction of the environment and for the loss of culture of the Cree. The James Bay Agreement made the Cree a self-administering nation, and they gained some temporary economic growth, but at the same time they signed away all hopes of ever experiencing economic development. The Cree who signed the Agreement in 1974 testified that they regretted signing the document.[1] The Cree felt that not only were they pushed into signing the agreement and were given little on paper, their bitterness extended to broken promises that have still not been filled.

When Europeans began to take over the newly "discovered" country centuries ago, something happened that they did not expect: the First Nations Citizens did not vanish. With the implementation of all the white man's laws, First Nations Citizens did not assimilate. Doris Ronnenberg, President of the Native Council of Canada, states that "in modern Canada, the fact is, the aboriginal population is growing at four times the rate of the general population ... [while] English and French populations are becoming increasingly out-numbered by other ethnic populations."[2] Politically, the Cree and other First Nations are becoming more active and more visible on the national and international front, indicating that they are not ready to assimilate. They strongly believe that "the Creator placed them here," that they have a right to this land, "unlike the English and French immigrants."[3]

During the past two decades, Canada has been faced with a new dilemma, one that should have been dealt with long ago: there is no longer only one group within the confederacy that wishes to be recognised as independent, there are several. Québec has been fighting for more autonomy since the battle at the Plains of Abraham. First Nations Citizens were so repressed that they never had the chance to demand control of their land. They spent the past few decades trying to regain the culture that they lost.

But now, they are gaining force and have made self-government their goal. One is tempted to say that there are two groups fighting for autonomy in Canada, but in fact the First Nations are just that, a group of several nations, and Québec is one nation.

A truly unique situation exists in Québec. The First Nations are fighting for autonomy within a nation that is struggling for the very same thing. Canada's image has been tarnished in the international community. Canada is suffering economically from the political uncertainty. This struggle, which has now entered the phase of constitutional debate, must be resolved as quickly as possible. Canada has to stop spending money on discussions which never have an outcome. It is truly in Canada's best interest to solve the demands for autonomy as quickly as possible.

According to many participants of these discussions, there are some new attitudes that are required in order to achieve an agreement. Former Chief of Alexander First Nation, Allen Paul, emphasises the importance of having an open mind: "We want to recommend to the general public and to all levels of government that you have to keep an open mind. You have to take those blinders off. You can't look at just one side. You have to look at it from all perspectives, if this situation is going to work."[4] Negotiators and other Canadians must keep their minds open to different possibilities, to invent perhaps a new form of power-sharing. "The concept of power-sharing is an important one and critical to a resolution of the grave problems confronting First Nations. The starting point for discussions about power-sharing arrangements must be premised on mutual respect and good faith. We have witnessed all too clearly that this is not the case in Canada,"[5] said Dick Martin, Executive Vice-President of the Canadian Labour Congress. People must understand that sharing responsibilities does not necessarily mean a decline in life-style. Canada has been decentralising, giving more power to the provinces. One must think of what would happen with a little more decentralising that included First Nations.

Much of the fight is over whether First Nations are in fact nations, and whether they have a right to the land they claim. Once they were considered nations, when Europeans took the time to sign treaties with representatives of these nations. The Canadian constitution was in fact derived from the "constitution" of the Iroquois Confederacy. Canadians do not wish to give First Nations self-government, for they fear that they lack the skills to govern themselves. It is true that the century of dependence has reduced some of the skills of First Nations Citizens, but one must not forget that before whites arrived, they governed themselves successfully. Ronnenberg states that "self-government and self-determination was the natural state of affairs for the aboriginal people of Canada for at least 39,800 of the last 40,000 years at even the most conservative archaeological estimates."[6]

It is time to reach a solution regarding the domination of First Nations. It is obvious that assimilation is not part of the future. The melting pot does not work, and it is time to start something different. Perhaps a new form of power-sharing with First Nations across the country and with Québec would provide a better sense of living in a multicultural society. Ethnic groups are fighting among one another; new solutions must be discovered, and these will only be reached with open minds.

What are the possible solutions for peripheral regions? The dependency theory outlines two possibilities: revolution and delinking. A revolution is quite unlikely for First Nations Citizens. Delinking, however, is recommended by Samir Amin as a possible solution to the world problem of Third World countries. As explained in the first chapter of this book, delinking is not a complete cut from the central economic system, but it is an "awareness" of self-development. Samir Amin explains that "the meaning is as follows: pursuit of a system of rational criteria for economic options founded on law of value on a national basis with popular relevance, independent of such criteria of economic rationality as flow from the dominance of the capitalist law of value operating on a world scale."⁷ Delinking does not mean a complete break from the centre, since this is impossible, and Samir Amin acknowledges this point. However, the periphery must seize the chance to become more autonomous whenever the opportunity presents itself. Third World countries can only gain autonomy through self-development, as opposed to development from the centre. The economic decisions that need to be made must come from the people of the periphery and not economists in the centre. The economic decisions must make sense and improve the survival of the people in these underdeveloped regions.

As mentioned earlier, delinking does not mean a complete alienation from the centre; however, it involves an awareness of one's needs. By gaining control over their political, social, and economic situation, the peripheries will, over time, gain self-sufficiency. There would still be a contact between underdeveloped countries and the centre, but the trade that would occur would hopefully be more fair. For example, technology is something that cannot be exchanged on an equal level, but Samir Amin indicates the healthy attitude that peripheries must acquire.

> Delinking does not imply rejection of all foreign technology, simply for being foreign, in the name of some culturalist nationalism. But it certainly does imply an awareness that technology is not neutral, either in terms of social relations of production, or in terms of models of living and consumption, priority given to the involvement of the whole country, the entire people, in the process of change dictates a mix of modern technologies (possibly imported) and renovation and improvement of traditional technologies."⁸

In truth this delinking is what the Cree and the other First Nations in Canada are fighting for: self-determination. Like Third

World countries, the First Nations are trapped by colonisation, loss of culture, debt, and social problems. These peripheries need economic and social development in order to stop being peripheries. First Nations believe that they will only progress if they have self-government or self-determination.

The next section will discuss what members of the First Nations believe self-government will bring to them, what is needed to have self-determination, and what exactly self-government is.

Self-Determination

Self-government is the First Nations' solution to dependency. They believe that delinking will lead to development for them. James Frideres outlines four points that summarise what the First Nations hope to gain by self-determination:

1. Greater self determination and social justice. Protection of and control over one's own destiny, rather than subordination to political and bureaucratic authorities based outside the ethnic group.

2. Economic development to end dependency, poverty, and employment. Economic justice in the sense of a fair distribution of wealth between the aboriginal and non-aboriginal populations.

3. Protection and retention of aboriginal culture.

4. Social vitality and development that will overcome such existing social problems as ill health, the housing crisis, irrelevant and demeaning education and alienation.[9]

First Nations representatives believe that in order to achieve these goals they need the following: 1) political institutions that would be accountable to the aboriginal electorate; 2) a territorial base; 3) control over group membership; and 4) continuing fiscal support.[10]

Much of the debate over self-government has concerned the lack of a definition. The federal government and the provinces refuse to grant anything to the First Nations without having a clear picture of what they mean by self-determination. In an attempt to define the term self-government and to discuss how self-determination could be implemented, leaders of the First Nations have met on several occasions. During the "proceedings of a conference held September 30 - October 3, 1990," David Joe, a land claims negotiator for the Council of Yukon Indians, attempted to define the extent to which First Nations would like to control their destinies. David Joe discusses the laws they would like to make for themselves:

The Schedule would detail those subjects under which Indian governments might exclusively make laws, these being:

- the form of government;
- conditions for citizenship in the Indian Nations;
- the administration of justice and its enforcement, and adjudication;
- the regulation of domestic relations, including marriage, divorce, illegitimacy, adoption, guardianship, and support of family members;
- the regulation of property use;
- economic development, including trade and commerce;
- social programs, including the health, education, and welfare of members of First Nations.[11]

First Nations are suggesting a form of government that would be more powerful than a municipal government, with powers similar to that of the provinces. They simply want more control over their lives.

First Nations would like the right to tax their residents; however their residents should be exempt from federal and provincial taxes. This proposition is met with much opposition, because many feel that First Nations Citizens would enjoy all the freedoms of self-government, benefit from federal funding, and at the same time pay no federal or provincial taxes. In other words, in the view of some, they would enjoy freedoms at the expense of other Canadian taxpayers. But who is to say, if they had more control over their lives, whether the crime rate would decrease, or whether the welfare and unemployment rates would decrease, or whether their health would improve? An unhealthy society would cost more to taxpayers than First Nations that are healthy and functioning well in their society.

There are two more areas of debate concerning the First Nations' need for self-government. The first concerns First Nations Citizens living off reserves, in rural areas, and the second debate concerns First Nations women. Many outside the Native community have said that self-government could never work outside the reserves. Some have given the example of a First Nations Citizen being arrested in downtown Toronto, alleging that the police officers could not arrest the Native person because that person is under a different legal jurisdiction, and so on. However, First Nations representatives assure the rest of the population that this would not happen. The laws they would include in the definition of self-determination would be minor and relate more to laws not concerned with crime. If there were to be laws related to criminal activity, they would deal with the levels of punishment rather than determination of what was criminal.

The second area of debate concerns First Nations women. During the talks on self-government, First Nations representatives have expressed their wishes to write their own charter of rights. Women are anxious, because they are not well-represented in these discussions. Women are afraid that they will lose the rights they have under the *Canadian Charter of Rights.*

There are only two First Nations in Canada that have a signed agreement for self-government: the Cree of James Bay and the Sechelt of British Columbia. "*The Sechelt Indian Band Self-Government Act* was passed in 1986. The Sechelt Indian band consists of 33 reserves located approximately 50 kilometres north of

Vancouver along the cost line."[12] Frank Cassidy and Robert L. Bish agree, in their book entitled *Indian Government Its Meaning in Practice*, that the Cree have more power of self-determination than do the Sechelt because the James Bay and Northern Agreement was accompanied with a comprehensive land claim. However, the following is also the case:

> Under the *Cree-Naskapi (of Québec) Act* and the *Sechelt Indian Band Self-Government Act*, for example, the bands concerned have been given a wide range of law-making powers, which permit them to exercise authority over numerous matters that directly affect them. The governing *Acts* take precedence over other federal laws in the case of conflict, and band laws similarly prevail over provincial laws that are inconsistent with them.[13]

Despite these acts, the First Nations remain dependent on the centre, because the centre controls all of their natural resources, thereby obstructing First Nations' economic development. "Finally, Natives argue that the present structural arrangement between them and the Government is paternalistic and contributes to the continuing dependency of Natives."[14]

As there are external and internal causes to the crisis that has been examined in this book, there are also internal and external solutions. Politicians need to listen hard to the needs and demands of the First Nations. They need to work laboriously to increase their creativity. New solutions must be found, and the problems will only begin to be resolved with the participation of both groups working toward the same goals. What harm could come to the other citizens of this country in recognising First Nations Citizens for what they are (members of the First Nations inhabiting what is now Canada)? As mentioned earlier, if returning self-government to First Nations Citizens will make them healthy,

Canada will be better off in several ways. For example, crime rates will decrease with a fair justice system which is adapted to cultural differences; welfare and unemployment rates will decrease with adequate school systems and economic development; our tax dollars will no longer be spent on constitutional talks and meetings which are very expensive and where no decisions are made; and finally, perhaps over the generations this process will ease the racial tensions that exist in this country.

But what of the question that began this book: Can one compare a First Nation in Canada to a Third World country? The conclusion reached after this examination is yes, one can compare the two quite well. But there are also differences. As each nation and country is unique, so are the Cree of James Bay. However, there are enough similarities to do a comparative analysis. All Third World nations have fought or are still fighting colonization. All Third World countries are dependent on the North, which in this case happens to be the centre. All Third World countries are plagued with grave socio-economic problems. Both Third World nations and First Nations are influenced by internal and external factors. Finally, both are in great need of a break from the cycle of dependency.

If the leaders in Canada and around the world ever open their minds enough to accept new solutions, and if these leaders ever get creative enough to envision new forms of power sharing, then perhaps the problems related to dependency will be resolved. But, until then, the negative effects of dependency will only continue to grow.

Notes

1. Richardson, Boyce. *Strangers Devour the Land*. Douglas and McIntyre Ltd., Vancouver, 1991, p.336.
2. Cassidy, Frank. *Aboriginal Self-Determination*, Oolichan Books and The Institute for Research on Public Policy, Winnipeg, 1991, p.37.
3. Ibid.
4. Ibid., p.80.

5. Ibid., p.84.
6. Ibid., p.36.
7. Amin, Samir. *La faillite du développement en Afrique et dans le Tiers-Monde.* L'-Harmattan, Paris, 1989, p.2.
8. Ibid., p.4.
9. Frideres, James S. *Native Peoples in Canada: Contemporary Conflicts.* Prentice-Hall, Scarborough, 1988, p.359.
10. Ibid.
11. Cassidy, Frank. *Aboriginal Self-Determination*, p.74.
12. Frideres, James S. *Native Peoples in Canada: Contemporary Conflicts*, p.361.
13. Cassidy, Frank. *Aboriginal Self-Determination*, p.45.
14. Frideres, James S. *Native Peoples in Canada: Contemporary Conflicts*, p.361.

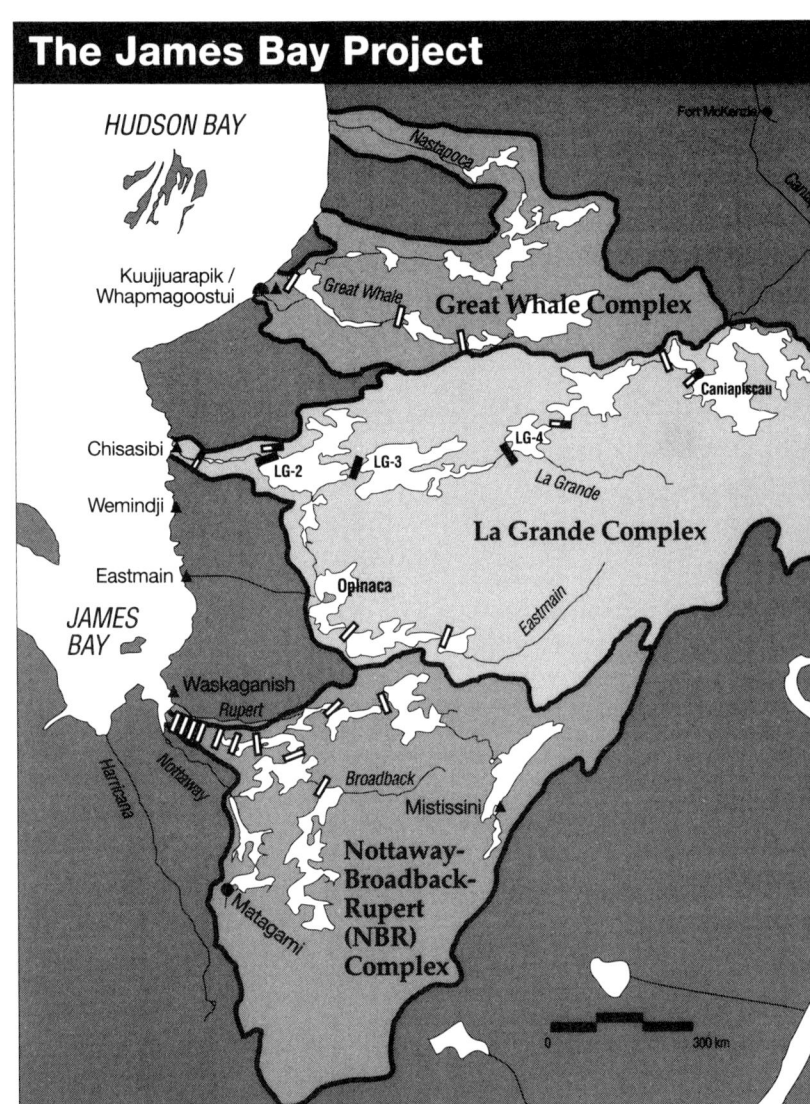

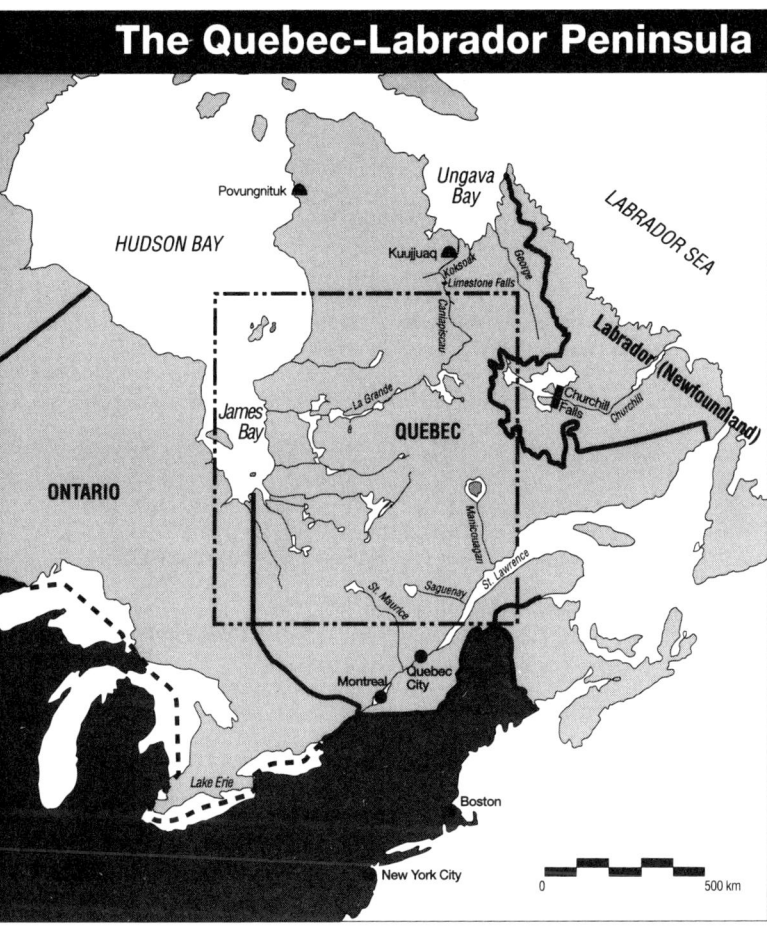

Bibliography

Adams, Howard. *Prison of Grass: Canada from a Native Point of View*. Fifth House Publishers (1975), Revised Edition, Saskatoon, 1989.
Akwesasne Mohawk Council, Kahnawake Mohawk Council & Tyendinaga Mohawk Council. *Mohawk Government Position Paper on Aboriginal Rights and the Canadian Constitution*. St. Regis: Akwesasne Mohawk Council, 1986.
Affaires Indiennes et du Nord. *Les Indiens du Canada: Québec et les provinces Atlantiques*. Ottawa, 1973.
Allahar, Anton L. *Sociology and the Periphery: Theories and Issues*. Garamond Press, Toronto, 1989.
Amin, Samir. *La faillite du développement en Afrique et dans le Tiers-Monde*. L'Harmattan, Paris, 1989.
Banque Mondiale. *Rapport sur le développement dans le monde 1990. La Pauvreté Indicateurs du développement dans le monde*. Oxford University Press, Washington, D.C., 1990.
Bartlett, R.H. *Indian Reserves in Quebec*. Studies in Aboriginal Rights, no.8, University of Saskatchewan Native Law Centre, Saskatchewan, 1984.
Batson, Wendy. "Bombs to Blackboards." *The New Internationalist*. no.179, January 1988:22-23.
Beaulieu, Denis. *The Crees and Naskapes of Quebec: Their Socio-Economic Conditions*. Direction des Communications du Governement du Québec, 1984.
Been, Melissa. "The Enemy Within." *The New Internationalist*. no.179, January 1988:18-20.
Behind the Image. Series Paths of Development, (Video) CIDA, 1985.
Berger, Thomas R. *Liberté fragile: Droits de la personne et dissidence au Canada*. (1981) Editions Hurtubise HMH Ltée, Ville de la Salle, Québec, 1985.
Blomstrom, Magnus and Bjorn Hettne. *Development Theory in Transition: The Dependency Debate and Beyond: Third World Responses*, Zed Books Ltd., London, 1984.
Boaz, Franz. *Kwakiutl Ethnography*. The University of Chicago Press, Chicago, "1966." (original date unpublished).
Boaz, Franz. *The social Organization and the Secret Societies of the Kwakiutl Indians*. Johnson Reprint Corporation, U.S.A., "1970" (original date unpublished).
Bourdieu, Pierre. "Les modes de domination." *Le sens pratique*. Aux éditions de Minuit, Paris, 1980.
Bourdieu, Pierre. "L'Objectivité du Subjectif." *Le sens pratique*. Aux éditions de Minuit, Paris, 1980.
Bourgeault, Ronald. "Women in Egalitarian Society." *One Sky Report: Native Women The Doubly Denied*. Regina, Summer, 1983:3-8.
Brazier, Chris. "Death of an Incorruptible Man." *The New Internationalist*. no.179, January 1988:6.
Brazier, Chris. "Running for Rights: A New Internationalist Olympics." *The New Internationalist*. no.179, January 1988:4-6.
Brecher, Irving (ed.). *Human Rights, Development and Foreign Policy: Canadian Perspectives*. The Institute for Research on Public Policy, Halifax, Nova Scotia, 1989.
Brightman, Robert A. *Acoohkiwina and Acimowina: Traditional Narratives of the Rock Cree Indians*. Canadian Ethnology Service, Mercury Series Paper 113, Canadian Museum of Civilization, 1989.
Brody, Hugh. *Maps and Dreams: Indians and the British Columbia Frontier*. Douglas & McIntyre, Toronto, 1988.

Bromley, D.F. Rosemary, and Ray Bromley. *South American Development: A Geographical Introduction*. Cambridge University Press, Cambridge, 1988.

Canadian International Development Agency. *Annual Report 1989-90*. Ministry of Supply and Services Canada, 1991.

Cassidy, Frank. *Aboriginal Self-Determination*, Oolichan Books and The Institute for Research on Public Policy, Winnipeg, 1991.

Cassidy, Frank and Robert L. Bish. *Indian Government: Its Meaning in Practice*. Institute for Research on Public Policy, Halifax, 1989, 1990.

Chalk, Frank and Kurt Jonassohn. *The History and Sociology of Genocide: Analyses and Case Studies*. Yale University Press, London, 1990.

Champagne, Linda. "Under Fire at Akwesasne." *Akwesasne Notes*. vol. 22, no. 2, Early Summer 1990:3-4.

Chance, Norman A. *Summary Report: Developmental Change among the Cree Indians of Quebec*, Rural Development Branch, Ottawa, August, 1970.

Chapdelaine, Claude. "Un site du Sylvicole moyen ancien sur la plage d'Oka (BiFm-1)." *Recherches amérindiennes au Québec*. vol. XX, no.1, 1990:19-35.

Chavez, Cesar (ed). *Food and Justice*. United Farm Workers, vol. 7, no.1, January 1990.

Choquette, Jerome (Minister of Justice). *The Administration of Justice Beyond the 50th Parallel*. Quebec, 1972.

"Church Official Backs Blockade to Protest Casinos on American Indian Land." *Akwesasne Notes*. vol. 22, no. 1, Late Spring 1990:21.

Churchill, Ward (ed.). *Marxism and Native Americans*. (1983) South End Press, Boston, 1989.

Clatworthy, Stewart J. *Issues Concerning the Role of Native Women in the Winnipeg Labour Market*. Institute of Urban Studies, University of Winnipeg, Winnipeg, May, 1981.

Clement, Wallace. "A Political Economy of Regionalism in Canada." *Structured Inequality in Canada*. John Harp and John R. Hofley (eds.), Prentice-Hall, Toronto, 1980.

Clement, Wallace. *Class, Power and Poverty*. Mathew Publications, Toronto, 1983.

Cleroux, Richard. "Quebec Police to Fort Chimo to maintain order in Eskimo protest against language." *Globe and Mail*. August 23, 1977:1.

Colden, Cadwallader. *The History of the Five Indian Nations: Depending on the Province of New York in America*. Cornell University Press, Ithaca, New York, 1973.

Cox, Peter. "Sweetness and Plight." *The New Internationalist*. no.189, November, 1988:13-14.

Cree Housing Corporation. *Cree Housing and Infrastructure Program: Five-year Capital Works Program 1979-1984*. Rupert House, March, 1980.

"Crisis at Kanesatake and Kahnawake: The Fundamental Issues." *Akwesasne Notes*. vol. 22, no. 3, Late Spring 1990:12-13.

Cumming, Peter A. and Neil H. Mickenberg (eds.). *Native Rights in Canada*. (2nd ed.), The Indian-Eskimo Association of Canada in association with General Publishing, Toronto, 1971.

Daniels, R. "Research Papers on the Implications of Treaty 8." Edmonton: Indian Association of Alberta, n.d.

Darnell, Frank. "Indigenous Cultural Minorities – Consepts pertaining to their education." *The Education of Minority Groups – An Enquiry into Problems and Practices of Fifteen Countries*. Organisation for Economic Co-operation and Development, Grower, Hampshire, England, 1983.

Davis, Frederick. "OPP in riot gear turn up at bingo game, standoff at Six Nations Indian Reserve." *Globe and Mail*. July 14, 1986:A13.

Days of Future Past. Series: Paths of Development, (Video) CIDA, 1985.

Debbane, Charlotte. "The Rule of the 'Warriors'." *Akwesasne Notes*. vol. 22, no. 1, Early Summer 1990:5.

Delâge, Denys. "L'alliance franco-amérindienne 1660-1701." *Recherches amérindiennes au Québec*. vol. XIX, no. 1, 1989:3-15.
Delâge, Denys. *Le Pays renversé: Amérindiens et Européens en Amérique du Nord-Est: 1600-1664*. Boréal, Compact, Québec, 1991.
Demmert, William G. "An American Indian View on Education for Indigenous Minorities." *The Education of Minority Groups — An Enquiry into Problems and Practices of Fifteen Countries*. Organization for Economic Co-operation and Development, Grower, Hampshire, England, 1971.
Dwyer, Augusta. "The Trouble of Great Whale," *Equinox*, no. 61, February, 1992:28-41.
Dyck, Noel (ed.). *Indigenous Peoples and the Nation-State: 'Fourth World' Politics in Canada, Australia and Norway*. Institute of Social and Economic Research, St-John's, Newfoundland, 1985.
Elliott, Jean Leonard (ed.). *Minority Canadians 1 — Native People*. Prentice Hall, Scarborough, Ontario, 1971.
Falconer, Patrick. *Urban Indian Needs: Federal Policy Responsibility and Options in the Context of the Talks on Aboriginal Self-Government*. (unpublished), Winnipeg, March, 1985.
"Federal Offical Denounces Warrior Society as 'a Gang of Criminals'." *Akwesasne Notes*. vol. 22, no. 3, Late Spring 1990:5.
Francis, Daniel and Toby Morantz. *Partners in Furs: A History of the Fur Trade in Eastern James Bay 1600-1870*, McGill-Queen's University Press, Kingston and Montreal, 1983.
Frideres, James S. *Native Peoples in Canada: Contemporary Conflicts*. Prentice-Hall, Scarborough, 1988.
Fortin, Gerard L. et Jacques Frennette. "L'acte de 1851 et la création de nouvelles réserves indiennes au Bas-Canada en 1853." *Recherches amérindiennes au Québec*. vol. XIX, no. 1, 1989:31-37.
Fumoleau, René. *As Long As This Land Shall Last: A History of Treaty 8 and Treaty 11, 1870-1939*. Toronto, McClelland & Stewart, 1976.
"Ganiengehaga: A Short History of the Mohawk People." *Akwesasne Notes*. vol. 8, no. 4, Late Autumn 1976:32-35.
Gauthier, Bernard. "Evaluation des interventions gouvernementales en matière d'éducation au Nouveau-Québec inuit." Recherches amérindiennes au Québec. vol. XIX, no. 1, 1989:63-81.
George, Susan. *Jusqu'au Cou: Enquette sur la Dette du Tiers Monde*, Editions La Découverte, Paris, 1988.
George, Susan. "Several Pounds of Flesh." *The New Internationalist*. no.189, November 1988:18-19.
Glewwe, Paul and Jacques Van der Gaag. "Identifying the Poor in Developing Countries: Do Different Definitions Matter?" *World Development*, vol.18, no. 6. Pergamon Press, 1990:803-814.
Goddard, John. *Last Stand of the Lubicon Cree*. Douglas & McIntyre, Toronto, 1991.
Goldman, Irving. *The Mouth of Heaven: An Introduction to Kwakiutl Religious Thought*. John Wiley and Sons, Toronto, 1975.
Grand Council of the Crees (of Quebec). *Annual Report 1988-1989*. Cree Regional Authority, May, 1990.
Grescoe, Paul. "A Nation's Disgrace." *Health and Canadian Society Sociological Perspectives*, Second Edition, Fitzhenry & Whiteside, Markham, 1987:127-140.
Hall, Thomas D. "Is Historical Sociology of Peripheral Regions Peripheral?" *Studies in Political Economy a Socialist Review: Rethinking Canadian Political Economy*. no.6, Autumn 1981.
Harrington, Micheal. *The Development of Underdevelopment: Why Poor Nations Stay Poor*. Simon & Schuster, a Division of Gulf & Western Corporation, 1977.

Haudenosaunee Confederacy. *Statement of the Haudenosaunee concerning the constitutional framework and international position of the Haudenosaunee confederacy*. St. Regis, Quebec, n.d.
Hawkes, David C. *Aboriginal Peoples and Government Responsability: Exploring Federal and Provincial Roles*. Carleton University Press, Ottawa, 1991.
Hawthorn, H.B. (ed.). *A Survey of Contemporary Indians of Canada*, Indian Affairs Branch, Ottawa, 1966.
Hoogvelt, Ankie M.M. *The Sociology of Developing Societies*. MacMillian, Publishers Ltd., London, 1985.
Hull, Jeremy. *Native Women and Work: Summary Report of a Winnipeg Survey*. Institute of Urban Studies, Winnipeg, March 1983.
Hunt, Constance. "Fishing Rights for Inuit Women." *Bulletin*. Canadian Association in Support of Native Peoples. Fall, 1978.
Indian and Northern Affairs Canada. *Health of Indian Women: Notes on Socio-Demographic Conditions*. Ottawa, 1990.
Indian and Northern Affairs Canada. *James Bay and Northern Quebec Agreement Implementation review*. Ottawa, 1982.
Indian and Northern Affairs Canada. *Supplementary I: Briefing Notes on the James Bay Health Crisis and Epidemic*. Ottawa, 1981.
Janigan, Mary. "Lonely Cries of Distrust: Anger and Pain Fuel Native Claims." *Maclean's*, vol. 105, no. 11, March 16, 1992:22-24.
Jaraham, Shekar. "Pacific Apartheid." *The New Internationalist*. no.179, January, 1988:18.
Jones, Dorothy M. *Urban Native Men and Women: Differences in Their Work Adaptations*. ISEGR Occational Papers, no.12, Institute of Social Economic and Government Reseach, University of Alaska, Fairbanks, Alaska, April, 1976.
Knight, Roff. *Ecological Factors in Changing Economy and Social Organization among the Rupert House Cree*. Anthropology Papers National Museum of Canada, Department of the Secretary of State, Ottawa, no.15, March, 1968.
Lafitte, Michel. "Les origines de la Confédération de Six Nations." *Les cahiers de gauche socialistes*, Dossier: La crise Autochtone. vol. 1, no. 1, Automne 1990.
Laprairie, Carol. "Native Women and Crime: A Theoretical Model." *The Canadian Journal of Native Studies*, VII, 1, 1987:121-137.
L'Art de tourner en rond. realisation: Maurice Bulbulian, production: Raymond Gauthier, (Video) L'Office Nationale du Film.
Larusic, Ignatius E. *Negotiating a way of life: Initial Cree experience with the administrative structures arising from the James Bay agreement*. Policy, Research and Evaluation Group, Research Division, Indian and Northern Affairs Canada, Ottawa, 1979.
Leacock, Stephen. *The Dawn of Canadian History: A Chronicle of Aboriginal Canada*. Glasgow, Brook and Company, Toronto, 1915.
Lefort, Claude. *Essais sur le politique: XIXe - XXe siècles*, Seuil, Paris, 1986.
Legros, Dominique. "Communautés amérindiennes contemporaines: structures et dynamique autochtones ou coloniales?" *Recherches amérindiennes au Québec*. vol. XVI, no. 4, 1986-1987:47-68.
Lelièvre, Sylvain. "Thèses sur la souveraineté des nations autochtones." *Les cahiers de gauche socialistes*, Dossier: La crise Autochtones. vol. 1, no. 1, Automne 1990.
Locke, Patricia. "An Ideal school System for American Indians — A Theoretical Construct." *The Schooling of Native America*. American Association of Colleges for Teacher Education, Washington, D.C., 1978.
Loslier, Sylvie. "Sessions de sensibilation aux actochtones a la Sûreté du Québec: Semer le doute." *Recherches amérindiennes au Québec*. vol. XVI, no. 4, 1986-1987:85-89.
Lydekker, John Wolfe. *The Faithful Mohawks*. Ira J. Friedman Inc., Port Washington, Long Island, N.Y., 1968.

Justice for All. Series Paths of Development, (Video) CIDA, 1985.
Mander, Jerry. *In the Absence of the Sacred: The Failure of Technology and the Survival of the Indian Nations.* Sierra Club Books, San Francisco, 1991.
Martin, Russell. *A Story that Stands like a Dam: Glen Canyon and the Struggle for the Soul of the West.* Henry Holt and Company, New York, 1989.
Mathews, Ralph. "Regional Differences in Canada: Social Versus Economic Interpretations." *Social Issues: Sociological Views in Canada.* D. Forcese and S. Richer (eds.) Prentice Hall, Toronto, 1982.
McAfee, Kathy. "IMF, World Bank, U.S. Aid in the Caribbean." *NACLA Report on the Americas.* vol XXIII, Number 5, Febuary 1990:14-40.
McBride, Catherine and all. *Charateristics of Public Administration Employment On-Reserve 1986 Census.* Quantitative Analysis and Socio-demographic Research, Working Paper Series 90-2, Finance & Professional Services, Indian & Northern Affairs Canada, August, 1990.
McCutcheon, Sean. *Electric Rivers: The Story of the James Bay Project,* Black Rose Books, Montreal, 1991.
McDonald, Arthur. "Why do Indian Students Drop Out of College?" *The Schooling of Native America.* American Association of Colleges for Teacher Education, Washington, D.C., 1978.
McGhee, Robert. *Beluga Hunters: An Archeological Reconstruction of the History and Culture of the MacKenzie Delta Kittegaryumiut.* Memorial University of Newfoundland, University of Toronto Press, Toronto, 1974.
Miller, J.R. *Skyscrapers Hide the Heavens: A History of Indian-White Relations in Canada.* Revised edition, University of Toronto Press, Toronto, Buffalo, London, 1991.
Miller, J.R. (ed.). *Sweet Promises: A Reader on Indian-White Relations in Canada.* University of Toronto Press, Toronto, 1991.
Mohawk Council of Akwesasne and Mohawk Council of Kahnawake. *Declaration of intent on Mohawks\ self-government, self-determination.* St-Regis, Quebec: 1986.
Mohawk, John. "Indian Economic Development: The U.S. Experience of an Evolving Indian Sovereignty." Unpublished, 1990.
Morna, Collen Lowe, "Learning for a Living." *Third World.* no.23, December 1989:57.
Morse, Bradford (ed.). *Aboriginal Peoples and the Law: Indian, Métis and Inuit Rights in Canada.* Revised first edition, Carleton Library Series, Carleton University Press, Ottawa, 1991.
Mukela, John. "Food and Flames." *The New Internationalist.* no. 189, November 1988:21.
"New York State Cases Involving Illegal Gambling Within Haudenosaunee Territories." *Akwesasne Notes.* vol. 22, no. 1, Late Spring 1990:21.
"Observers Hope for Peace at Akwesasne." *Akwesasne Notes.* vol. 22, no. 1, Late Spring 1990:20.
"Officer Cross cleared of killing Indian by Montreal jury." *Globe and Mail.* November 22, 1980:4.
"Oka Crisis Far From Over Kanesatake Stands Firm While Kahnawake Roadblocks Come Down Peacefully." *Akwesasne Notes.* vol. 22, no. 3, Late Spring 1990:5.
O'Neil, John D. "Health Care in Central Canadian Arctic Community." *Health and Canadian Society Sociological Perspectives,* Second Edition, Fitzhenry & Whiteside, Markham, 1987:141-158.
Ontario Native Womens Association. *Breaking Free: A Proposal for Change to Aboriginal Family Violence.* Thunder Bay, Ontario, December, 1989.
"Oppression of Native Women by U.S. and Canadian Laws." *Akwesasne Notes.* Fall, 1982.
Ozienwicz, Stan. "Cree, Eskimos contend Quebec language bill could break James Bay Pack." *Globe and Mail.* May 6, 1977:8.

Paikeday, Thomas M. (ed.). *Compact Dictionary of Canadian English*. Holt, Rineheart and Winston of Canada Limited, Toronto, 1976.
Parnell, Ted. *Barriers to Education*. Yukon Association of Non-Status Indians, Whitehorse, Yukon, 1976.
"Plans for Bingo on [Six Nations] reserve is heading for run-in with law." *Globe and Mail*. July 10, 1986:A18.
Philpot, Robin. *Oka: dernier alibi du Canada anglais*, Etudes Québecoises, Montréal, 1991.
Pryor, Edward T. *Profile of Native Women: 1981 Census of Canada*. Statistics Canada, Minister of Supply and Services Canada, Ottawa, February, 1984.
Publié pour le Programme des Nations Unis pour le développement, *Rapport Mondial Sur le développement humain 1990*. New York, 1990.
Quantitative Analysis and Socio-Demographic Research. *1986 Census Highlights on Registered Indians: Annotated Tables*. (DIAND) Minister of Supply and Services Canada, 1989.
Ray, Douglas and al. "Lifelong Education: An Emerging Human Right." *Human Rights in Canadian Education*. Kendall/Hunt Publishing Co., Dubuque, Iowa, 1983.
Richardson, Boyce. *Strangers Devour the Land*. Douglas & McIntyre Ltd., Vancouver, 1991.
Rohner. "The Kwakiutl: Indians of British Columbia," *Minority Canadians 1 - Native People*, Prentice Hall, Scarborough, Ontario, 1971.
Rose, Mike. "Escape from Torture" *The New Internationalist*. no.179, January 1988:10-11.
Roxborough, Ian. *Theories of Underdevelopment*. The Macmillan Press Ltd., London, 1983.
Ruttan, Vernon W. "Why Foreign Economic Assistance?" *Economic Development and Cultural Change*. vol.37, no.2. The University of Chicago, 1989: 411-424.
Sacouman, James R. "The 'Peripheral' Maritimes and Canada-Wide Marxist Political Economy." *Studies in Political Economy a Socialist Review: Rethinking Canadian Political Economy*. no.6, Autumn 1981:135-151.
Savard, Remi and Jean-René Proulx. Canada: dernière l'épopée, les autoctones, L'hexagone. Montréal, 1982.
Shaw, Florence. "[Six Nations] organizer vows to defy bingo raids." *Globe and Mail*. July 23, 1986:A16.
Shaw, Sue. "Dicing with Debt the Third World Dilemma." *The New Internationalist*, no.189, November 1988:8-9.
"Shots Shatter Night at Akwesasne." *Akwesasne Notes*. vol. 22, no. 3, Late Spring 1990:5.
Smith, Donald B. *Le auvage pendant la période héroïque de la Nouvelle-France (1534-1663) d'après les historiens Canadiens-Francais des XIXe et XXe siecles*. Colection Cultures amériendiennes. Cahiers du Québec/Hurtubise HMH, Musée nationaux du Canada-Musée national de l'homme, Ottawa, 1979.
Sotsisowah. "Ganienkeh." *Akwesasne Notes*. vol. 8, vol. 4, Late Autumn, 1976:36.
"'SS' Blasted by Mohawk Nation." *Akwesasne Notes*. vol. 22, no. 1, Late Spring 1990:21.
Stanbury, W.T. *The Education Gap: Urban Indians in British Columbia*. University of British Columbia, Vancouver, 1973.
Swift, Anthony. "Moonlight, Bulldozers and the Honeypot." *The New Internationalist*, no.189, November 1988:8-9.
Tanner, Adrian. *Bringing Home Animals: Religious Ideology and Mode of Production of the Mistassini Cree Hunters*, Social and Economics Studies No. 23, Institute of Social and Economic Research, Memorial University of Newfoundland, C. Hurst & Co. (Publishers) Ltd., London, 1979.
Taylor, Debbie. "Black Land, White Land." *The New Internationalist*. no.179, January 1988:13-14.

Thatcher, Richard. "Stop Stealing Our Children." *Canadian Dimension*. Winnipeg, October/Novermber, 1982.
"The Joe Anderson Gambling Operation at Tuscorora." *Akwesasne Notes*. vol. 22, no. 1, Late Spring 1990:22.
Thordarson, Bruce. *Banking on the Grass Roots*. The North-South Institute, Ottawa, 1990.
Teevan, James J. (ed.). *Introduction to Sociology: A Canadian Focus*. second edition, Prentice-Hall Canada Inc., Scarborough, Ontario, 1986.
"Tribes Mediator Proposes Truce; Two Chiefs Walf Out Before it's Discussed." *Akwesasne Notes*. vol. 22, no. 1, Late Spring 1990:20.
Turner, Janice. "Death on Delivery." *The New Internationalist*. no.189, November 1988:20-21.
United Nations Development Program. UNDP. *United Nations Development Program World Development Annual Report*. 1990.
United Native Nations. *After the ink dries: Will promises made be promises kept: Concerning James Bay Agreement Alaska Settlement, proposed CODE agreement*. Vancouver: n.d.
Van Wyk, Chris. "Breaking the Spirit." *The New Internationalist*. no.179, January 1988:13-14.
Veltmeyer, Henry. "The Underdevelopment of Atlantic Canada." *Review of Radical Political Economics*, vol.10, no.2, 1978.
Wadden, Marie. *Nitassinan: The Innu Struggle to Reclaim their Homeland*, Douglas & McIntyre, Toronto, 1991.
Walens, Stanley. *Feasting with Cannibals: An Essay on Kwakiutl Cosmology*. Princeton University Press, 1981.
"'Warriors' Confront Sûreté du Québec at Akwesasne." *Akwesasne Notes*. vol. 22, no. 3, Late Spring 1990:3.
"What the Other Media Said ... " *Akwesasne Notes*. vol. 22, no. 2, Early Summer 1990:6-9.
White, Pamela M. *Native Women: A Statistical Overview*. Social Trends Analysis Directorate and Native Citizens Directorate, Department of Secretary of State, Ottawa, September, 1985.
White, Richard. *The Roots of Dependency: Subsistance, Environment, and Social Change among the Choctaws, Pawnees and Navajos*. University of Nebraska Press, London, 1983.
Wills, Richard H. *Conflicting Perceptions: Western Economics and the Great Whale River Cree*, Tutorial Press, 1984.
Wilson, Roger. "Teachers for Indian Children." *The Schooling of Native America*. American Association of Colleges for Teacher Education, Washington, D.C., 1978.
Wolcott, Harry F. *Case Studies in Education and Culture: A Kwakiutl Village and School*. Holt, Rineheart and Winston, Toronto, 1967.
Wright, J.V. *Quebec Prehistory*, National Museum of Man, Van Nestrand Reinhold Ltd., Toronto, 1979.
York, Geoffrey. *The Dispossed: Life and Death in Native Canada*. Vintage U.K., London, 1990.
York, Geoffrey, and Loreen Pindera. *Peoples of the Pines: The Warriors and the Legacy of Oka*, Little, Brown & Company, Toronto, 1991.
Young, T. Kue. "The Health of Indians in Northwestern Ontario." *Health and Canadian Society Sociological Perspectives*, Second Edition, Fitzhenry & Whiteside, Markham, 1987:109-126.

Index

accidents, 69
acculturative stress, 131
Alberta Indians; franchise, 85; incarceration, 83
alcoholism, 71, 75, 76, 77, 81, 129-130; childbirth defects, 77; fetal alcohol syndrome, 77; history, 75-76; incarceration, 84; *Indian Act*, 86-87; prevention, 131; residential schools, 76; violence, 70
Algonkin, 29
alienation, 46-47
autonomy, 143; lack of, 15
Awashish, Phillip, 117, 118
Bearskin, Job, 109, 110
Berger, Thomas, 104
Bill of Human Rights, 86-87; Section 27, 87
Blair, Judge William, 71
Bobbish, James, 131
Bourassa, Robert, 115, 116, 117, 120, 124, 134
British Columbia Indians; incarceration, 83; Sechelt, 146
Brown, Mandy, 71
Canadian Charter of Rights, 146
Cardoso, Fernando Henrique, 8
Casanova, Pablo Gonzalez, 17
centre and periphery; synonyms, 8-9
Chilcote, Ronald H., 8
Chomsky, Noam, 15, 89
Chrétien, Jean, 120
Clarke, Derek, 71
class; and dependency, 19; landless, 18; merchant, 18, 38-39
Clement, Wallace, 21
colonizers; France, 33-34; England, 33-34; Holland, 33-34
Compagnie du Nord, 42-43
Coon-Come, Mathieu, 123, 128
conservations; beaver, 40-41
Cree; alienation, 46-47; band names, 30; dialect, 29; hunting camp leader, 32; hunting cycle, 30-31; hunting territories, 31-32; land ownership, 32-33; religion, 32; social organisation, 31, 40
Cree-Naskapi (of Quebec) Act, 147
Cross, James, 115
culture; broken, 45, 55; caught between two, 76; genocide, 95; loss of, 95, 140; protection, 144; retention, 144

death rates, 69
debt, 39
delinking, 23-24, 142-143
denationalized, 18
dependence; colonial, 12; financial-industrial, 12; new, 12; technological-industrial, 12
dependency; and class, 19; definition, 10; effects, 3; external (definition), 14; internal (definition), 14; regional, 13-14, 15
dependency theory; application in Canada, 20; definition (introduction), 2-3; definition (Dos Santos), 7-8; origin, 8
development; stages, 12
Diamond, Billy, 118, 120, 132
diffusionists, 6
Dos Santos, Theotonio, 8; new dependence, 12; stages of development, 12
dualists, 6
economy; development, 67, 81, 144; growth, 67, 68, 140; justice, 144; world, 38
Edelstein, Joel, 8
education; beneficial, 96-97; control, 122-123; federal schools, 55; harmful, 96-97, 100; history, 43-44; informal, 95, 97, 99; Kwakiutl, 97-100; mandatory, 46, 55; propaganda, 96-97, 100
electricity, 112; conservation, 133-134; negawatts, 133-134
employment, 56
endogenous factors, 15
energy; negawatts, 133-134; surplus, 116
Energy Corporation, 115, 118, 119, 127
erosion, 127
exogenous factors, 15
Faletto, Enzo, 8
feudalism, 18
financial aid; government transfer payments, 55, 59, 60; social assistance cheques, 55; welfare cheques, 55, 59
Fornazzari, Dr. Juis, 80
franchise, 85
Frank, André Gunder, 8
Front de Libération du Québec(FLQ), 115
Furtado, Celso, 8
Galeano, Eduardo, 13

gasoline sniffing, 77-80; juvenile crimes, 78; prevention, 77, 79; rates, 78; sudden sniffing death syndrome, 79
genocide; cultural, 95
Hare, Kenneth, 30
health, 72; alcoholism, 77; cancer, 73; cavities, 130; childbirth defects, 77; children, 73; circulatory problems, 73; cirrhosis of the liver, 73; cultural gap, 74; death, 69; diabetes, 130; diarrhea, 132; diseases, 44-45, 72; fetal alcohol syndrome, 77; gastroenteritis, 72; housing, 72; income, 61; mercury poisoning, 74; nutrition, 61; obesity, 130; pneumonia, 72; programs, 56, 73; services, 73-74; sexually transmitted diseases, 130; sickness, 56; stillbirths, 73; teenage pregnancies, 130; tuberculosis, 72-73; women, 73
Heat and Power Consolidated, 114
heating system, 64, 67
Herman, Edward, 15, 89
housing; conditions, 56, 64-67; health, 72; heating system, 64, 67; homeless, 64; income, 61, 72; overcrowding, 56, 64-67; violence, 70
Hudson's Bay Company (HBC); founding, 35
human rights, 71-72
Hunters and Trappers Income Security Program, 123
hunting; camp leader, 32; cycles, 30-31; territories, 31-32; traplines, 129
Hydro Quebec; creation, 115-116; sales, 116
illiterate; functionally, 92

imperialist; theory, 7
incarceration, 83, 84
income, 57, 58, 59; health, 61, 72
Income Tax Act, 85-86
Indian Act, 56, 46, 66, 74, 104; Bill C-31:, 88, 89; creation of, 89-90; education, 94; Section 10:, 88; Section 12(i)(a)(iv):, 88; Section 12(1)(b):, 87-88; Section 12(2):, 88; Section 14:, 88; Section 29:, 85; Section 35:, 85; Section 73:, 85; Section 88:, 85; Section 94(b):, 86-87; Section 109:, 88

Indians of Quebec Association, 117, 118
Iroquois, 48, 89
James Bay Northern Quebec Agreement, 121, 124, 140; division of land, 121-122; health, 74; settlement, 120-123; signing, 121
James Bay Development Corporation, 118, 119
James Bay Project; appeal 119-120; creation, 114; debts, 116; description, 110-111; environmental conservation, 127; facilities, 113; history, 114-115; opposition, 124; roads, 112-113
Joe, David, 145
juvenile crimes, 78
Kwakiutl; education, 97-100
labour; cheap, 19
Laporte, Pierre, 115
land; damage, 125; erosion, 127; ownership, 32-33, 85, 121-122
Lévesque, René, 114
Levitt, Kari, 20
Lovelace, Sandra 87-88
Lovins, Amory, 133, 134
Lubicon Cree, 29
Lytton reserve, 71
Malouf, Justice Albert, 4, 118, 119-120
Manitoba Indians; alcoholism, 75, 76; gasoline sniffing, 78; incarceration, 84
marriage; restrictions, 41
Marshall, Donald, 82-83
Martin, Dick, 141
Marxists, 7, 11, 15, 47
Matthews, Ralph, 21, 22
McGill University, 118
Meech Lake Accord, 1
mercury agreement, 126
mercury poisoning, 74, 126-127, 128, 130
methylmercury, 126
Mianscum, François, 4
Montagnais, 29, 35
Montreal Light, 114
multinationals (MNC), 17-18, 20
myths, 96, 98-99
negawatts, 133-134
New Brunswick Indians; alcoholism, 75; franchise, 85; incarceration, 83
Newfoundland Indians ; incarceration, 83
Niosi, Jorge, 20, 21
Northern Quebec Inuit Association, 120

nutrition; cavities, 130; diabetes, 130; obesity, 130
October Crisis, 115
Ojibwa, 29
O'Reilly, James, 118, 132
overcrowding, 56, 64-67; violence, 70
Pachanos, Violet, 131
Parsons, 6
Paul, Allen, 141
police force, 83
policies; government, 46-47
Potts, Lillian, 100
poverty, 56
power sharing, 141, 142, 148
prices; goods, 60
Prince Edward Island Indians; franchise, 85
programs, 73; recreational, 79
Quebec Indians; franchise, 85
Quiet Revolution, 114
racism, 57
Readhead, George, 79
recommendation 141
recreation; programs, 79
regional dependency; Clement, Wallace, 21; Matthews, Ralph, 21, 22; Veltmeyer, Henry, 21
religion ; alienation, 46-47; Catholics, 44; Cree, 32; missionaries, 43-44; Protestants, 44
residential school syndrome, 95
resources; non-renewable, 58, 68
Revillion Frere, 43
Ronnenberg, Doris, 140
Rostow, 6
Royal Proclamation, 85
Sagasti, Francisco, 10
Saskatchewan Indians; alcoholism, 75, 76; incarceration, 83
schools, 101; federal, 55; residential, 71, 94-95, 97
Sechelt of British Columbia, 146
Sechelt Indian Band Self-Government Act, 146
self-determination, 143, 144, 145-147; description, 144; needs to achieve, 144; section, 144
self-development, 24, 143
self-government, 144, 146, 147; definition, 145; off-reserve, 146; taxes, 145; women, 146

self-reliance, 11, 49; delinking, 23
self-respect, 81
self-sufficiency, 24, 33, 48, 76, 96, 143
self-sustaining, 33
sexual abuse, 71
Shamattawa Cree, 5, 60, 62, 69, 81
Shawanda, Bea, 76
Shubenacadie, 73
Six Nations Confederacy of the Iroquois, 89
social change, 68
social evolutionists, 6, 15, 16
Spencer, 6
status; loss of, 46-47, 88, 94; women, 87-88, 89
St. George's School, 71
structures; internal (definition), 6; external (definition), 6; political, 89-90
sudden sniffing death syndrome, 79
suicide, 71
surplus; energy, 116
Tanner, Adrian, 32
Tenenbein, Dr., 81
trade; equal, 37-38; unequal, 35-37
trapping; restrictions, 41
Trudeau, Pierre, 115, 118
Turgeon, Justice, 119
underdevelopment; consequences, 22; synonyms, 10-11; vs undeveloped, 10-11
unemployment, 56; rates, 62; violence, 70
vegetation, 30
Veltmeyer, Henry, 21
violence, 56, 69-71, 81, 129; alcoholism, 77; unemployment, 70
Watts, Charlie, 120
welfare; alcoholism, 76; dependence, 56
wild life; caribou, 127; *ducks*, 127; *fish stocks*, 125; *geese*, 127
Wolpe, Harold, 17
women, 54-55; health, 73; incarceration, 83; income, 59; loss of status, 87-88; self-government, 146; suicide, 71; violence, 69-71
world-system theory, 8, 14, 19

Also published by

BLACK ROSE BOOKS

ELECTRIC RIVERS
The Story of the James Bay Project
Sean McCutcheon

...a book about how and why the James Bay project is being built, how it works, the consequences its building will have for people and for the environment, and the struggle to stop it...it cuts through the rhetoric so frequently found in the debate.
Canadian Book Review Annual

Electric Rivers *is a welcome contribution to the debate...a good fortune for readers who would like to better understand a story that is destined to dominate the environmental and political agenda in Québec and Canada for many years to come.*
Globe and Mail

194 pages, maps
Paperback ISBN: 1-895431-18-2 $18.95
Hardcover ISBN: 1-895431-19-0 $37.95

THE NEW RESOURCE WARS
Native Struggles Against Multinational Corporations
Al Gedicks

Aboriginal and environmental coalitions fighting against corporate greed and environmental racism is mirrored in hundreds of struggles all over the world, from James Bay, Québec to the Ecuadorian Amazon Rainforest. This new book documents these struggles and explores the underlying motivations and social forces that propel them. It concludes with a discussion of Native treaty rights and the next stage of the environmental movement.

250 pages, index
Paperback ISBN: 1-551640-00-7 $19.99
Hardcover ISBN: 1-551640-01-5 $38.99

WOLLASTON
People Resisting Genocide
Miles Goldstick
Foreword by Dr. Rosalie Bertell

The story of the Natives' struggle in northern Saskatchewan to protect their homes from the effects of uranium mining.

These are important issues, and in raising them Goldstick does us a service.
Border/Lines

315 pages, photographs, illustrations
Paperback ISBN: 0-920057-95-0 $16.99
Hardcover ISBN: 0-920057-94-2 $36.99

Send for our free catalogue of books
BLACK ROSE BOOKS LTD.
C.P. 1258, Succ. Place du Parc
Montréal, Québec H2W 2R3 Canada

Printed by the workers of
Les Éditions Marquis
Montmagny, Québec
for Black Rose Books Ltd.